IF YOU
CAN'T SAY
ANYTHING
NICE,
SAY IT IN
YIDDISH

IF YOU CAN'T SAY ANYTHING NICE, SAY IT IN YIDDISH

THE BOOK OF YIDDISH INSULTS AND CURSES

LITA EPSTEIN

FALL RIVER PRESS

Fall River Press
122 Fifth Avenue
New York, NY 10011

ISBN: 978-0-7607-8673-4

Printed and bound in the United States of America

10 9 8 7 6 5 4 3 2

Contents

IF YOU
CAN'T SAY
ANYTHING
NICE,
SAY IT IN
YIDDISH

1

From Secret
for Survival
to Worldwide
Language

Yiddish is the language that helped Jews survive when being persecuted in Europe and Russia during numerous periods, starting with the First Crusades in 1096. This secret language only understood by Jews allowed them to communicate and transact business outside the earshot of their persecutors. By the time of the Holocaust, ten to eleven million Jews spoke Yiddish worldwide and it was the most widely spoken Jewish language.

Half of the Jews who spoke Yiddish were killed during the Holocaust. Few of those who suffered the horrors of the Holocaust wanted to pass the language on to their children because it was so tied to Eastern Europe and unhappy memories. Instead, most Yiddish speakers wanted to assimilate with their new language and home—primarily in the United States. So the use of Yiddish gradually died off.

Today it's estimated that only one to two million people speak Yiddish fluently and they can be found primarily in the Orthodox Jewish communities of New York, Chicago, Miami, Toronto, Los Angeles and Israel. Hebrew is the official language of Israel. In fact, at first Israel banned the use and study of Yiddish, but that changed in the 1960s and 1970s.

Luckily the language does survive today and there is also a resurgence of interest in Yiddish and its culture—its music, theater and literature. Many believe the only way one can truly understand the lives and culture of Jews in Eastern Europe and Russia during the period before the Holocaust is to learn Yiddish and read the stories, poetry and plays written during that period.

I'll talk more about that in Chapter 3. First I'll review how Yiddish got started and how it grew into the language of the East European Jews up to the time of the Holocaust.

Where Yiddish started

Someone didn't get up one morning and say it's time to start a new language. Yiddish gradually built into a language over hundreds of years. Most historians believe Yiddish started to flourish sometime in the Middle Ages between 900 and 1100. Before that time Jews in Europe were speaking a Jewish dialect of Old French and Old Provencal. Early Yiddish included words from the Romance languages, as well as Hebrew, but today three quarters of Yiddish words find their basis in German.

The language developed primarily among the Jews who escaped the First Crusades and moved north to the German lands, which at the time was called Ashkenaz by the Jews, Ashkenaz being the Hebrew word for Germany. Descendants of these Jews are called Ashkenazi Jews.

There was another group of Jews that never learned Yiddish: Sephardic Jews. Sephardic Jews, from Spain and

Portugal, took a different path to get away from the persecutions in Europe and moved to Syria, Egypt and other Middle Eastern communities. They were never influenced by the German language and never learned Yiddish.

Now back to the Jews who went North. These Jews who settled along the Rhine River spoke a Jewish-French dialect known as Laaz. They started incorporating German words, primarily from an early form of medieval German, known today as Middle High German. In fact some German scholars today are learning Yiddish because there are more Middle High German words in Yiddish than in modern German. Hebrew words also found their way into everyday Yiddish.

As Jews continued to live in the German lands, the language they spoke gradually became known as Jewish, which meant Yiddish in German. That's how Yiddish became the name for the new language. The first recorded use of this term was found in 1597. The word itself is related to the German word for Jewish, which is Judisch. Germans called the Jews *ein Jude*. Yiddish speakers call a Jew Yid and a non-Jew a goy.

But long before Yiddish was named as a language, it became widely spoken among the Jews. By the 13th century the new language had made such inroads among the Jewish population that it replaced both Hebrew and the local Christian languages in daily conversation. Yet there was still much respect for the Hebrew language, and translation of the Torah, the Jewish name for the Old Testament and its related writings, into Yiddish was discouraged.

Yet books were written in Yiddish, but featured a disclaimer saying they were primarily for women, who were considered the uneducated. Few women received Hebrew training at that time. For this reason, Yiddish became a women's language and the name mam'eh loshn (mother tongue) is maintained for Yiddish even today. Yet, don't make the mistake of thinking men didn't use it. It was the primary language of business.

Women who did receive training in Hebrew translated many of the Hebrew prayers into Yiddish, embellishing them for women at the same time as well. Many of the women's Yiddish prayers were embellished with additional thoughts that focused on family and community. These prayers focused on the matriarchs of the Jews—Sarah, Rebecca, Rachel and Leah. Prayers in Hebrew are primarily focused on the patriarchs—Abraham, Isaac and Jacob.

Moving east splits the language

In the 13th century the Jews were forced by persecution to move again. They moved to eastern Germany, Poland and other Eastern European territories. Yiddish was then exposed to the Slavic languages, primarily Lithuanian, Polish and Ukranian. Words from those languages are still found in Yiddish today.

Yiddish then divided into two dialects: Western and Eastern Yiddish. The Western dialect was spoken primarily in Germany, Holland, France, Switzerland and Hungary. The Eastern dialect was spoken in Eastern Europe. But speakers of both dialects could understand each other. The differences between these two dialects were primarily heard in pronunciation, much like the differences in accents between the North and the South in the United States.

It wasn't until the 16th century that Yiddish became a written language. The language was written using Hebrew characters, but vowels were added to make it easier to read. When you see Yiddish today, you usually see Yiddish written using transliteration. I do use transliteration in this book. That's actually the Yiddish written out according to sound equivalents in English. In this book I primarily use YIVO Yiddish transliteration, which was developed by the YIVO Institute for Jewish Research. There are other Yiddish transliterations, which is why you will see Yiddish words spelled differently sometimes, but the original Yiddish using Hebrew lettering is all the same. I show you some basics of transliteration in chapter 4.

Finding a home in Poland

The Polish kings welcomed the Jews and encouraged them to work as merchants, traders and bankers. They liked the Jews because they had no ties to the Polish political system and could be used as political pawns. The Jews maintained a separate social place, somewhere between the Polish landowners and the peasants. Since the Jews had their own language, they kept pretty much to themselves outside of business dealings. Jews preferred to use Yiddish, as well, and doing so allowed them to keep a separate society.

The Jews were happy not to be persecuted. The Poles enjoyed the Jews' trading contacts with other parts of

Europe. The Jews served as buying agents for the nobility. They maintained, produced and distributed staples, including wheat, wine, sugar, lumber and fur. Serving as middlemen, the Jews deflected the peasants' ire from the landowners, which helped as well.

For the first time, the Jews in Poland had a sense of stability and were allowed to control their own communities. The Jewish communities were built around Jewish law and tradition, including their own religious-run educational system. Yiddish helped the Jewish community construct its unique and private way of life. So everyone benefited.

Peace did not last long though because the Jewish communities in Poland became pawns, as control of Polish lands switched back and forth between Polish kings and Russian nobility. Persecution started again, but Yiddish held the community together and gave the community the ability to communicate privately amongst themselves.

Yiddish also flourished in Eastern Europe as a language for theater, music and literature written about the Jewish culture at the time. In fact, Yiddish is a language of culture unlike any other language today. All other languages have a country base. For Jews, Hebrew is a language of country—Israel.

This book looks at the humorous side of Yiddish—the curses and insults. Not the kind of stuff that grandparents normally would teach their children. Since it is against Jewish law to curse other Jews, you'll find Jews got very creative with how they cursed others. Many of the more direct curses you'll find in the book were developed in modern-day usage. The Jews of Eastern Europe were probably more likely to use the longer, more descriptive curses and insults you'll find in this book.

Acknowledgments

Many of the phrases I used in the book were gathered by numerous Yiddish scholars over hundreds of years. One of the most famous of these scholars was Sholem Aleichem, whose Yiddish stories are still read today. They are the source of at least one play you've probably seen—*Fiddler on the Roof.*

A good source for finding these Yiddish blessings and curses is Yosef Guri, whose book *Let's Hear Only Good News: Yiddish Blessings and Curses* was published by the Hebrew University of Jerusalem.

2

You Too Speak Yiddish and You Might Not Even Know It!

Let's set the stage. Imagine you're standing in line at a bagel shop in just about any major city in the United States. You overhear the discussion between two women as they decide what they want to eat and shmooze about personal news and friends:

SARAH: So, what are you going to eat?

HANNAH: I think I'll get lox and a shmear of cream cheese on a bagel.

SARAH: I don't know if I'm that hungry. Maybe I'll just get a nosh.

HANNAH: So, nu?

SARAH: Did you hear that shmuck Isaac asked Lisa for a date?

HANNAH: Oy vay, he's such a klutz.

SARAH: So what are your plans for the weekend?

HANNAH: I'm going to see the new play at the Yiddish theater. I hear the shtik is hysterical.

SARAH: Sounds like fun. Unfortunately, I'm moving into my new apartment so I have to shlep lots of stuff across town and won't have time.

Do you realize there are ten Yiddish words in that short scene? Most people don't even realize they are actually speaking Yiddish. Words that find their basis in Yiddish above include: *bagel, shmooze, lox, shmear, nosh, nu, shmuck, oy vay, shtik and shlep.* Just in case you haven't heard them or are not sure of their English meaning, here's the scoop:

- **Bagel:** Probably one of the most popular Jewish foods that has found its way into many American hearts, is a hard, ring-shaped bread roll that finds its beginnings in Yiddish with German origins. The official Yiddish word is *beygl* from the Middle High German word *bougel.*

- **Lox:** Smoked salmon from the Yiddish word *laks,* which means salmon. This actually comes from the German word for salmon, *lachs,* which was taken from an Indo-European word meaning salmon.

- **Shmooze:** To engage in casual conversation, many times in order to gain an advantage or make a social connection. This word comes from the Yiddish word *shmuesn* with a basis in either *shmues* (chat) or *schmue* (rumor).

- **Shmear:** In this conversation it means to use a dab of cream cheese on the bagel, but you will also hear *shmear* used when people talk about buying a bunch of things together, such as "She bought the whole shmear." The actual Yiddish word is *schmir*, which means smear or smudge, from the word *shmirn* or grease, which stems from the Middle High German word *smiren,* also meaning to smear or grease. When not used in the context of eating, shmear can mean the whole works or to be excessively kind for selfish gains.

- **Nosh:** A light snack or light meal. This comes from the Yiddish word *nash* or *nashn,* which means to eat sweets or to nibble on food. The basis for this Yiddish word can be found in the Middle High German word *naschen,* which means to nibble.

- **Nu:** A commonly used Yiddish slang for "What's new?" but has many other uses as well. It can also be used as a question, such as "*Nu?* When does he show up?"; to show impatience, such as "*Nu!* What was said?"; to dare someone, "*Nu,* prove it to me!"; or to just make a strong statement, "*Nu,* I told you so!"

- **Shmuck:** A clumsy or stupid person. This comes from the Yiddish word *shmock,* which means penis or fool, but some think its beginnings are actually in the Polish word *smok,* which means serpent or tail.

- **Oy vay:** Means Oh, no, but in Yiddish actually means Oh, pain. People also use it to say things like "How terrible," "That's horrible."

- **Shtik:** An entertainment routine, usually a comedy act. This comes from the Yiddish word *shtik,* which means piece or routine, but has its origins in the High Middle German word *stucke* or piece.

- **Shlep:** A Yiddish word that means to drag an object with difficulty. It can also be used to describe a long, tedious or difficult journey. For example, "Wasn't that trip to the city a *shlep?*" It comes from the Yiddish *shlepn* and its origin is the German word *schleppen*, which means to drag.

Yiddish at your breakfast or dinner table

Food makes up a large part of every Jewish family get-together. Every Jewish holiday has its collection of favorite foods. So it's not surprising that a lot of Yiddish words regarding foods have made it into everyday language. Here are some of the most common words:

- *Bialy:* A roll, shaped like a disc, that is thicker around the outer edges and flattened in the middle. The middle of a *bialy* is traditionally filled with onion pieces and sometimes cheese. It gets its name from the Polish city Bialystok, which is credited with its creation.

- *Blintz:* One of my favorite breakfast foods—looks like a thick crepe or thin pancake that's folded around some type of filling. Cheese, potatoes and fruit, individually or combined, are the most common fillings used. This comes from the Yiddish word *blintse*, which finds its origins in the Russian word *blinets* or "little pancake."

- *Gefilte fish* (ge-*fil*-teh): Nope, there is no such thing as a *gefilte* fish swimming around in the ocean. I can remember my mother spending hours making *gefilte* fish before a major holiday. She even had a special bowl and chopping tool for making it. It's actually made by starting with a whole fish, then chopping it into very small pieces. Most often, whitefish, carp or pike and sometimes salmon is used, and sometimes a mixture of more than one of these types of fish. Other common ingredients include: onions, celery, carrots, sugar, white pepper, salt, eggs and matzo meal. The mixture is then stuffed back into the fish's skin or body cavity (bones and all) and boiled or baked. Today, most people just buy balls of gefilte fish mixture in jars or cans, and you will find it on the dinner table at all Jewish holiday celebrations. The Yiddish word *gefilte* literally means "stuffed fish."

- *Halvah:* Claimed not only by the Jews, but also by many Middle Eastern cultures. It originated in the Balkans and eastern Mediterranean regions. It's made using sesame seeds and honey or sugar syrup. Other ingredients can be added, such as: dried fruit, pistachio nuts and almonds. Some people add cinnamon and cardamom. The ingredients are blended together, heated and poured into bars or loaves. In addition to the Yiddish word *halvah*, Turkish call it *helva*, Greeks call it *halva*, Arabs call it *halwa* or *halawi*. In each case it translates to "sweetmeat."

- *Kaiser roll:* A breakfast roll that is light and fluffy on the inside with a thin outer crust. It's made by using a square piece of dough and folding the corners of the dough into the center. Sometimes it's made with poppy seeds and sometimes without seeds. The name for this roll actually comes from Germany, called *Kaisersemmel* for the German emperor, plus *semmel*, which means roll.

- ***Knish*** (k-nish): A piece of dough stuffed with potato, meat or cheese and baked or fried, commonly eaten as a snack or an appetizer. The Yiddish word *knish* comes from the Ukrainian word *knysh*.

- ***Kosher:*** Means conforming to dietary laws, when talking about food. Its route is Hebrew, and means fitting or proper. Today as a slang term, it's used when talking about nonfood items and means that the material is legitimate, permissible, genuine or authentic. For example, it's commonly used in phrases such as: "Using bikes on the path is *kosher,*" or "The story about New York is *kosher.*"

- ***Kugel:*** Traditionally it's made with noodles or potatoes, baked with eggs and seasoning. A sweet kugel is common as well, and is made with noodles, raisins and apples. In Yiddish, *kugel* actually means ball, which related to its puffed-up or mound shape. The word originates in Middle High German.

- ***Rugelach*** (ru-*ge*-lach): A crescent-shaped cookie made from a cream-cheese dough filled with jam, chocolate, cinnamon, sugar or nuts, or some combination of these ingredients, cut into a triangle and rolled up. My mom could never make them fast enough when we were growing up. They were eaten as soon as they came out of the oven.

- ***Shmaltz*** and ***shmaltzy:*** When talking about food, it relates to something greasy, gooey or with a lot of fat drippings. But, you'll also hear it when someone is talking about something corny or overly sentimental. In that case a "y" is added at the end. For example,

"Wasn't that a *shmaltzy* play?" Some people also use *shmaltzy* to describe something as flattery, sweet talk or overpraise. For example, "Wasn't that a *shmaltzy* introduction?" The word comes from the Yiddish word *smalts*, which literally means "melted fat," which is originally from the German word *schmalz* of the same meaning.

- **Traif:** Means forbidden food and not prepared by the rules of Jewish dietary laws. It's the opposite of "kosher." You may hear this word also used for non-food items, such as books or movies, that are forbidden. For example, "Don't go to see *Deep Throat* [a pornographic flick]—it's *traif.*"

Yiddish for when you need that special expression

- **Feh:** Can serve as a multipurpose word. Use it when you want to say "Fooey!"; "That's terrible!"; "I hate that!"; "That stinks!"; or "How disgusting!"

- **Gevalt** or **Oy gevalt** (ge-*valt*): Use it when you hear shocking news. It's usually used to express alarm, dismay, fear, terror or astonishment. When used with "oy," it can mean "That's dreadful!" or "Holy shit!" It comes from the Yiddish expression *G'vald*, which literally means force or violence.

- **Gezunt-heit** (ge-*zunt*-heit): Means good health. Commonly used when someone sneezes, sometimes in conjunction with "God bless you." You can also use it as part of a toast.

- **Gottenyu** (*got*-ten-yu): Use it to express despair, anguish or to show pity for something. It's a substitute for "Oh, God!"

- **Megillah** (me-*gil*-lah): When someone blows something way out of proportion, you can call it a big *megillah*. It's also used to say that someone has told you the entire story with complete details—many times in a very longwinded way. The word actually is the name of the story of Esther and read on the holiday of Purim.

- **Plotz** (*plots*): When you feel like you are ready to explode from too much excitement or anger, you can say, "I want to *plotz*." It means to burst.

- **Shalom** (*sha*-lom): A Hebrew word with lots of different meanings, including, hello, peace, good-bye, so long and other similar words of welcome when someone comes in or good-bye when someone leaves. But it's only good-bye until you can welcome someone again.

- **Tough** *toches* (*too*-ches): Use when you want to say "Tough luck" or "Too bad." *Toches* is another word for butt, ass, backside or fanny. You get the idea.

- **Shandeh** (*shan*-deh): Use when you are embarrassed about something or think something is a shame. For example, when you hear someone has just experienced a misfortune or embarrassment, you can say, "That's such a *shandeh*."

Yiddish for categorizing people and what they do

- **Bubbeh meisseh** (*bub*-eh *my*-seh): Use it when you think someone is telling you an old wives' tale or something completely unbelievable. It literally means a grandmother's story, but don't use it around your grandmother if she knows Yiddish, or she'll be pretty angry. It's usually used when you just don't believe what someone is telling you.

- **Chutzpah** (*chutz*-pah): Means a lot of nerve. This can be a good thing or bad thing. When you use it positively it means someone has a lot of nerve and daring. But negatively it can mean someone has a lot of nerve and has gone too far.

- **Emmes** (*em*-mes): Means truth or on the level. If you want to indicate that you believe something someone is telling you, you say that it's *emmes*.

- **Farblondjet** (far-*blond*-jet): When you think someone is totally confused, you can say they are *farblondjet*. Also used when you think someone is lost.

- **Farcockt** (far-*cocked*): When you think someone is full of shit, you can say, "you're *farcockt.*" It also means shitty or badly soiled.

- **Farmisht** (far-*misht*): When you think someone is all mixed-up or confused, another phrase you can use is "You're *farmisht*."

- **Kibbitz** and **Kibbitzer** (*kib*-itz and *kib*-itz-er): When someone talks too much or gets involved in a subject when they shouldn't, they're called a *kibbitzer*. *Kibbitz* usually means to give unsolicited or unwanted advice. A person that offers that advice is a *kibbitzer*, also known as a meddlesome spectator.

- **Koved** (*ko*-vid): When you hold high respect for someone or something, you are said to *koved* it. *Koved* means respect, honor, revere or hold in high esteem.

- **Kvell:** Used when you are gloating over your children, showing pride in their accomplishments. Someone might also *kvell* when they are enjoying an enemy's bad luck.

- **Maven** (*may*-vin): When you think someone is an expert, you can call him a *maven*. Also used to indicate someone is an authority on a subject, or a connoisseur.

- **Mazel** or **Mazel tov** (*ma*-zel): *Mazel* in Hebrew means luck. *Tov* is the word for good. Also used to say "Congratulations!"

- **Mensch:** Someone who does good works and helps others is called a *mensch*. Literally it means person or human being. Use this word when you want to give others the impression that someone is truly worthy of respect for his good deeds, would make a good husband or business partner, treats others fairly and meets his obligations.

- **Mitzvah** (*mits*-veh): Means a good deed. When you do something to help someone else, it's called a *mitzvah*.

- **Naches** (*nach*-es): Means joy or happiness. Used most often by parents to say their children give them great *naches*.

- **Nudnik** (*nood*-nik): If someone is badgering you and they are a very annoying person, you can call them a *nudnik*. Also used when someone is a bore, being obnoxious, nagging you or generally being a nuisance.

- **Nudge:** Means someone who pesters, annoys or complains persistently. It comes from the Yiddish word *nudjen,* which means to pester or to bore. Its actual origin is from the Polish word *nudzi,* which means the same.

- **Saichel** (*say*-chel): When you think someone is very smart or wise, you say they have *saichel.* This can also mean someone has common sense, tact or diplomacy.

- **Shmo:** If you think someone is a complete jerk or patsy, you can call him a *shmo.* It comes from the Yiddish word *shmok,* which means penis or fool.

- **Shnook:** When someone is easily victimized, in other words stupid, a sucker or a dupe, you can call them a *shnook.* The Yiddish word *shnook* is actually from the Lithuanian word *snukis,* which means mug or snout.

- **Shikker** (*shik*-er): Someone who is a drunkard is a *shikker.* This Yiddish word comes from the Hebrew word *sikkor* or *sakar* "to be drunk."

- **Tsores** (*sor*-es): When you have a lot of problems or troubles, you can say you are facing a lot of *tsores.* Also can be used to express misery.

Yiddish for when things just aren't right

- **Mishegass** (mih-sheh-*gas*): When everything is just crazy or has gone insane, you can call it a big *mishegass.* This is a variation of the Hebrew word *meshugga* (meh-*shu*-ga), which means crazy.

- **Mishmash:** When everything is a mess, you can call it a *mishmash.* Also fits when you think something is a hodgepodge or a jumble. It is believed this comes from the 15th century and was formed by a repetition of the word *mash*.

- **Shlok joint:** When you go into a store that sells cheap stuff, you can call it a "*shlok* joint." It means that something has no value or is junk. It comes from the Yiddish word *shlak*, which means stroke or evil. Its route is the Middle High German word *slag*.

- **Shmutz:** Means lots of dirt or slime.

3
The Yiddish Worldwide Revival

You may wonder how Yiddish survives today. During the Holocaust, half of the Jews who spoke Yiddish were killed. After the Holocaust, the language began to die off. Many Jews from Eastern Europe and Russia that escaped the Holocaust didn't want to have anything to do with the culture they left behind. Yiddish in Jewish homes in the 1950s to 1980s was spoken primarily by grandparents and few children were taught the language.

Many started to declare Yiddish a dying language and few anticipated the revival we are seeing today—a worldwide revival of Yiddish literature, music, radio, books and plays—that is gaining international momentum. Today, Yiddish is offered for study in more than fifty universities and there are more than fifty published Yiddish newspapers. Worldwide exchanges through Internet-based organizations keep the momentum growing.

Only about one to two million people still speak Yiddish today and you'll find them primarily in the Orthodox Jewish communities of Israel, New York, Chicago, Miami, Los Angeles and Toronto. But that's not the whole story.

Many groups are helping to revive the rich language and culture of Yiddish, which is really the only way to study the culture of the Jews of Eastern Europe in *mam'eh loshn* (the mother language). I'll review some of the top sources for finding more about Yiddish today.

YIVO Institute for Jewish Research

The YIVO Institute for Jewish Research in New York (www. yivoinstitute.org), which opened its doors eighty years ago, serves as the center of Yiddish scholarship. The institute was founded in 1925 in Vilna, Poland. It is the only pre-Holocaust scholarly institution to transfer its mission to the United States—a mission that fosters better understanding of the Eastern European roots of the American Jewish experience. YIVO's archives include a collection of more than twenty-two million letters, manuscripts, photographs, sound recordings, artworks and artifacts.

Today YIVO continues its mission that was started in 1925 by publishing scholarly books and journals, sponsoring academic conferences and courses in Yiddish language and literature, and sponsoring activities for the general public, including concerts, lectures and exhibitions. In 1995, YIVO was the cofounder of the Center for Jewish History, which is located at 15 West 16th Street in New York City. You can call the institute at 212-246-6080.

National Yiddish Book Center

The National Yiddish Book Center, located in Amherst, Massachusetts, was founded in 1980 by MacArthur Fellow

Aaron Lansky, who serves as president of the center today. He started his work when, as a twenty-three-year-old graduate student, he was alarmed to learn that throughout North America thousands of priceless Yiddish books, which had survived the Holocaust, were being discarded or destroyed. Children and grandchildren of Holocaust survivors, who no longer understood Yiddish, were tossing out books because they couldn't read the language.

Lansky took a two-year leave from graduate school and started what turned out to be his lifelong work—to save Yiddish books and the entire language from extinction. He sent out a public appeal for all Yiddish books that were unwanted. Working with a small group of people over the next six months, he rescued books from cellars, attics, synagogues and abandoned buildings. Within six months, Lansky and his crew had rescued 70,000 books. Today his library has over 1.5 million. Two of his largest finds include a 15,000-volume Jewish library that Lansky and his crew rescued from the basement of a demolished building in Bronx, New York, and 8,000 books that were left in a garbage Dumpster.

The extensive duplicate holdings of the center have helped to stock 450 Yiddish collections around the world, including libraries at Harvard, Yale, the U.S. Library of Congress, the British Library, Hebrew University of Jerusalem, as well as national libraries in Australia, China and Japan.

The National Yiddish Book Center is not only a collection of books. The center is probably best known for its popular thirteen-hour radio series, *Jewish Short Stories from Eastern Europe and Beyond*, which was done for

National Public Radio. In the summer months, it runs its annual Summer Program on Yiddish Culture. Its quarterly magazine, *Pakn Treger* (*Book Peddler*), has been called the best Jewish magazine in America.

You can access a large collection of the books saved by the center online at www.yiddishbookcenter.org. If you join the center for $36, you can also get its quarterly magazine. The center plans to scan and put all the books in its collection online as part of its Steven Spielberg Digital Yiddish Library.

Mendele

You'll find a lively exchange of views, information, news and just about anything else about Yiddish language and literature, if you subscribe to the Internet-based mailing list called Mendele (shakti.trincoll.edu/~mendele/index. utf-8.htm). The mailing list is moderated and subscriptions are free.

Mendele is a fictional character, a bookseller, from the works of Yiddish writer Sholem-Yankev Abramovitch. Mendele itself is like the pages of a Letters to the Editor section of newspapers with submissions of material of general interest. The owners of the list do moderate what is sent out and sometimes do minor editorial revisions. Mendele is distributed several times a week. In addition, subscribers get an e-mail of Personal Notices and Announcements regarding Yiddish-related events and commercial offerings.

The group also distributes a literary supplement called *The Mendele Review*, which reviews new and newly discovered Yiddish literature, and a theater review called the

Yiddish Theatre Forum. The list owners include Victor Bers (Yale University), Iosif Vaisman (University of North Carolina) and Noyekh Miller (Trinity College).

Folksbiene Yiddish Theatre

The longest-running Yiddish theatre in the United States is the Folksbiene Yiddish Theatre company (www.folksbiene. org), which has entertained audiences for over eighty-five years. It is the oldest continuous-running venue for Yiddish theater in the world and is one of the last of the Yiddish theaters that flourished in the first half of the century.

All productions are in Yiddish, but if you don't know the language, don't despair. You can rent earphones that permit you to hear simultaneous translations in Russian or English.

Living Traditions

Living Traditions (www.livingtraditions.org), founded in 1994, focuses on bringing Yiddish culture to contemporary Jewish life. Twenty years ago it started introducing Yiddish music, dance, history, folklore and crafts and visual arts through its KlezKamp, a weeklong program in which participants immerse themselves in the Yiddish folk arts. Living Traditions also offers classes, publications, recordings and documentaries.

The organization's executive director, Henry Sapoznik, was a coproducer of the Peabody Award-winning radio show *Yiddish Radio Project.* The show was a critically acclaimed ten-part radio series on the history of Jewish broadcasting that ran on National Public Radio's *All Things Considered* in the spring of 2002.

Jewish Theater

A global website that promotes Jewish theater and other performing arts worldwide is the Jewish Theater (www.jewish theater.com). The website strives to encourage an intercultural dialogue among Jewish communities worldwide using the Internet. The Jewish Theater also maintains a global network for professionals in the theater.

The website was started in December 2001 after a conference called "Toward a Vibrant and Coherent Theatre of the Jewish People," which included thirty Jewish theater directors and academics. The conference was held in Tel Aviv and was hosted by the Jewish Agency's People to People Center.

The website was spearheaded by Moti Sandak and is based on his ten years of research in Jewish theater. This includes a rare collection of plays and professional articles. The Jewish Theater also maintains connections with leading libraries and databases around the world. Information you can find on the website includes comprehensive and targeted coverage of the international community of Jewish theater. It serves as the leading source of industry news in the world.

The Workmen's Circle

Yiddish cultural life is inspired year-round by activities of The Workmen's Circle (www.circle.org), which has fostered both Jewish and Yiddish culture for over 100 years. The circle seeks to provide a connection to Yiddish culture and language and a broad knowledge and understanding of Jewish heritage. The circle sponsors year-round cultural events in various Jewish communities in the United States.

The California Institute for Yiddish Culture and Language

One of the leading groups for fostering the increased interest in Yiddish culture and language in the western United States is the California Institute for Yiddish Culture and Language (www. yiddishinstitute.org). The institute is a not-for-profit organization that provides intensive Yiddish learning programs, seminars and web-radio broadcasts.

The institute also assembles and disseminates a Living Yiddish Treasures DVD archive. Its programs are open to adults of all ages, and are offered in collaboration with other local academic and cultural institutions. The institute seeks to inspire and empower individuals to become Yiddish activists, educators, artists and writers.

Bar Ilan University Rena Costa Center for Yiddish Studies

The largest university program for Yiddish studies is at the Bar Ilan University Rena Costa Center for Yiddish Studies (www.biu.ac.il/JS/li/yiddish) in Israel. Over 200 students, ranging in age from twenty to eighty, attend Yiddish classes each year. The school also plans to offer courses on the Internet.

Rena Costa in establishing the center said, "If Yiddish dies, Hitler will have won, and that is a victory we must make sure he does not have."

Shortly after the establishment of Israel, Yiddish was banned because it was seen as the language of the ghetto and Hebrew was the primary language. Formal prohibitions against Yiddish entertainment were not lifted in Israel until 1960s and 1970s as the desire for Yiddish entertainment grew. Finally, in 1996 the Israel Knesset passed a law establishing a National Authority for Yiddish and allocated funds for the program.

The Forward

Once the most respected Yiddish daily newspaper, *The Forward* (www.forward.com) is still being published today in English, Russian and Yiddish. The newspaper was started in 1897 by Abraham Cahan and served as the voice of Jewish immigrants. In its heyday in the 1930s, the circulation was 275,000 copies and was read around the world. As Yiddish declined, so did the circulation of the newspaper, which was cut to a weekly in 1983. Today, with the revival of interest in Yiddish, the newspaper is again becoming a trusted guide to the Jewish experience.

Der Bay

Der Bay is an international Anglo-Yiddish newsletter (www. derbay.org). Its goal is to foster the preservation of the Yiddish language and the associated Yiddish culture, music, theater, literature and poetry via the International Association of Yiddish Clubs (IAYC). You'll find an extensive collection of links to Yiddish music, theater and literature on its website.

Ari Davidow's Klezmer Shack

You'll find an impressive collection of Yiddish music at Ari Davidow's Klezmer Shack (www.klezmershack.com). You'll find lists of Klezmer bands and their locations, as well as Yiddish radio shows you can access on the Internet. Ari Davidow also provides numerous Internet links to stores and equipment, music books, and Klezmer organizations and associations.

4

Now How
Do I Say
That?

Yiddish is predominatly a combination of German and Hebrew. Other languages are mixed in as well, including Aramaic, Polish, Ukranian and Lithuanian, as well as words from the Romantic languages, such as French.

This chapter will focus on the keys to pronouncing Yiddish words and understanding Yiddish sentence structure. Yiddish uses the Hebrew alphabet, but I won't be using that in this book. Instead I'll offer transliteration of that Yiddish, which is English lettering used to spell out Yiddish words according to sound equivalents. There are several different styles of Yiddish transliteration. I predominantly use YIVO, which was developed by the YIVO Institute for Jewish Research. In some cases I was only able to find the phrase as a transliteration, so the spelling may be different since I didn't have the original Yiddish to work with.

I've also included an additional version of each word or phrase to show you how to pronounce the word. Even that won't help without a bit more explanation. Probably the most difficult sound is the guttural version of "ch" that you'll find in words throughout Yiddish. Unless you've learned Hebrew or German, you probably are not familiar with the sound. If you've ever heard a German say "*achtung*" where the "ch" is pronounced by rolling the sound from deep inside the throat—that's how the "ch" should be pronounced.

Otherwise most of the pronunciations will be more familiar to you. Here's a basic chart based on the YIVO version of transliteration for some key vowels, consonants and sounds unique to Yiddish that you'll come across in the book:

Letters	Sound Equivalent
a	Pronounce like the *a* in father
o	Pronounce like the *o* in sort
u	Pronounce like the *u* in hut or put
oo	Pronounce like the *oo* in goo
ey	Pronounce like the *ey* in grey
ee	Pronounce like the *ee* in feet
oy	Pronounce like the *oy* in boy
ay or y	Pronounce like the *y* in sky
e	Pronounce like the *e* in end
ch	Pronounce with a guttural sound like the *ch* in "achtung"
ts	Pronounce similar to the *ts* in fruits

You will see *ayf, ahf* and *oyf* used throughout the phrases in the book. These words were used interchangeably in Yiddish, depending on how the author heard the original phrase, so don't worry about differences in meaning. I do include an English translation of all the words and phrases.

Many times when the letter *h* is added after a vowel, it is used as an indication that you need to stretch out the vowel. For example, when you see *ahf* that means to pronounce the *a* as you would in "harvest." When *h* is added to the end of the word, that means you should pronounce that vowel as a separate syllable.

In most cases when you see a word with two syllables, the accent falls primarily on the first syllable. Words of three or more syllables usually have the accent on the second syllable. I show where to put the accent by putting that part of the word or phrase in italics. Since Yiddish is made up of at least two dialects, and some say four, pronunciation can differ depending upon where the Yiddish phrase was first found. You will hear and see different accents among Yiddish speakers today.

5

How to
Hold a
Grudge—
Yiddish-Style

Now, let's look in on Sarah and Hannah as they have dinner at a Kosher restaurant on the Lower East Side of New York. Sarah was just fired by her boss and Hannah is trying to cheer her up and maybe help her vent some of her anger and frustration. . . .

HANNAH: *Nu?* What happened?

SARAH: (*sobbing*) Don't know. I was just working diligently at my desk and my boss stopped by and asked to see me in his office.

HANNAH: You had no idea what was coming?

SARAH: Nope, no warning. Here's a curse my mother would wish on him. "*Vifil yor er iz gegangn oyf di fis zol er geyn af di hent un di iberike zol er zich sharn oyf di hintn,*" which means, "As many years as he's walked on his feet, let him walk on his hands, and for the rest of the time he should crawl along on his ass." (Vi-fil yor er iz ge-*gang*-en oyf di fis zol er *geyn* af hi *hent* un di i-*ber*-ike zol er zich *sharn* oyf di *hint*-en.)

HANNAH: (*laughs loudly*) I can just see him walking on his hands, then crawling on his butt. He should have such pleasure for a long time.

SARAH: But, that one's too good for him. Maybe this one from my Uncle Louie is more appropriate. "*Got zol gebn, er zol hobn altsding vos zayn harts glist, nor er zol zayn geleymt oyf ale ayvers un nit kenen rirn mit der tsun.*" That means, "God should bestow him with everything his heart desires, but he should be a quadriplegic and not be able to use his tongue." (*Got zol geb-*en er zol *hob-*en *alts-*ding vos zhine *harts glist*, nor er zol *zayn* ge-*leymt* oyf ale *ay-*vers un nit *ken-*en rirn mit der *tsun.*)

HANNAH: Ha-ha. Now you're getting into the groove. And since your boss likes to think he's a big shot and meet with all those top politicians, let's throw in this curse from my uncle Harry. "*Me zol din aynladn tsum gubernator oyf a seydeh in du zolst im gebn a grepts in ponem arayn,*" which means, "May you be invited to a feast by the governor and may you belch in his face. (Me zol din ayn-*lad-*en gu-*ber-*na-tor oyf *sey-*deh in du zolst im gebn a *grepts* in *pon-*em a-*rhine.*)

SARAH: (*chuckles*) Nice one. I'd love to watch that one. I've got a better one. Since he's getting married next month, this curse from my aunt Sadie. "*Zoln verem praven a chaseneh in dayn boyn in aynladn ale zeyere kroyvim—fun inupets biz sladobke,*" which means, "May worms hold a wedding in your stomach and invite their relatives from all over." (Zoln *ver-*em *prav-*

en a *chas*-e-neh in dayn *boyn* in ayn-*lad*-en ale *zey*-ere
kroy-vim—fun in-u-*pets* biz *slad*-ob-ke.)

HANNAH: Love it. We can even join in on the dancing.

SARAH: Nope. Wouldn't want to dance at his wedding,
but my uncle Harvey likes this curse about dancing.
"*Zoln dayne shunim oyslenken zeyere fim ven zey
veln tantsn oyf dayn keyver.*" That means, "May your
enemies sprain their ankles dancing on your grave."
(Zoln *day*-ne *shun*-im oys-*len*-ken *zey*-ere fim ven zey
veln tants-en oyf dayn *key*-ver.)

HANNAH: Good one, but before we get away from that
stomach distress, how about this curse from my aunt
Esther? "*Sazol dir azoy dreyen boyd me zol meynen
az sayiz a katerinke,*" which means, "May your
innards turn and grind so much, people will think
you are an organ grinder." (*Sa*-zol dir a-zoy *drey*-en
boyd me zol *mey*-nen az *say*-iz a ka-*ter*-in-ke.)

SARAH: Yeah, and we should be sure to give him a
monkey as a wedding gift.

HANNAH: Ah, you're just being too good to him.

SARAH: (*giggles*) And of course we can't forget to think
about his new bride. How about this curse from my
aunt Ruthie? "*Zolst hobn di same fete gandz—nor kit
keyn tseyner di beste vayn nor nit keyn chushtem di
senste vayb—nor nit keyn zehrut.*" That means, "May
you have the juiciest goose—but no teeth; the best
wine—but no sense of taste; the most beautiful
wife—but be impotent." (Zolst *hob*-en di sa-*me fete
gandz*—nor kit *key*-en *tseyn*-er; di *bes*-te *vine*—nor nit

keyn chush-tem; di *sens*-te *vayb* – nor nit *keyn zeh-*
rut.)

HANNAH: That will make for some wedding night. Just
to be sure they enjoy their ride to the honeymoon,
let's throw in this curse from my uncle Abe. "*Zolst
azoy farfoylt vern az tsign, tchoyrn, un chazirim zoln
zid opzogn tsu forn mit dir in eyn fur*," which means,
"May you rot so badly that goats, skunks and pigs
will decline to travel in the same cart as you." (Zolst
a-*zoy far*-foylt vern az *tsign*, *tchoy*-ern un cha-*zir*-im
zoln zid op-*zog*-en tsu *forn* mit dir in eyn *fur*.)

SARAH: Okay, enough. My sides are aching from laugh-
ter. I never thought you'd be able to cheer me up. I
guess a few good Yiddish curses can help anyone
feel better.

Cursing in Yiddish can be both challenging and creative.
Since Jewish law decrees Jews cannot curse other Jews,
Yiddish curses over the ages have been developed as
backhanded blessings, and many are humorous to boot.

If you've seen the play *Fiddler on the Roof*, you've probably heard many of the curses Sholem Aleichem found as
he traveled worldwide collecting Yiddish curses and
insults for his writing. One of the most famous curses in
this play involves a scene in which the rabbi is asked if
there is a blessing for the czar. After thinking a while, the
rabbi says, "May God bless and keep the czar far away
from us."

In this chapter I focus on the Yiddish curses that Jews
used when they held a grudge against someone and wanted

them to suffer for a long time, sometimes past their own life span.

Wishing someone calamity, destruction, disaster and misfortune

May calamity strike you – *Eyn oyschapenysh zol oyf dir kumen* (Eyn oys-*chap*-ensysh zol oyf dir *kum*-en).

May calamity strike you and your filthy family – *A brod oyf dir un oyf dyn* (A *brod* oyf dir un oyf dyn).

May calamity strike you in the stomach [in your head; in your guts] – *A klog dir in boyd* [*in kop; in dyne podle kishkes*] (A *klog* dir in *boyd* [in *kop*, in *dyne pod*-le *kishk*-es).

May characters like you be sown thickly and germinate thinly – *Azoyne zol men kedicht zeyn in seeter zoln zee oyfgeyn* (A-*zoyne* zol men ke-*dicht zeyn* in *sit*-er zoln zee *oyf*-geyn).

May destruction strike you – *A churbn oyf dir* (A *churb*-en oyf dir).

May disaster strike you – *A klog zol dir trefn* (A *klog* dir *tref*-en).

May misfortune fall upon you – *Eyn umgleek oyf dir* (Eyn um-*gleek* oyf dir).

May misfortune strike you – *Eyn umgleek zol dir trefn* (Eyn um-*gleek* dir *tref*-en).

May misfortune strike your guts – *Eyn umgleek dir in kishkes* (Eyn um-*gleek* dir in *kishk*-es).

One misfortune is too few for him – *Eyn umgleek az far im veynik* (Eyn um-*gleek* az far im *vey*-nik).

Wishing someone a not-so-pleasant long life

May the Lord send a blessing for success to your pack of troubles – *A mazel-bracheh zol dir der eyberster tsores* (A *maz*-el *brach*-eh zol dir der ey-*best*-er *tsor*-es).

May suffering consume you – *Oysgefleekt zolstu vern* (Oys-*gef*-leekt *zols*-tu vern).

May you be as tormented in your death as I am in my life – *Zolst zid azoy matern mitn toyt vee in mater zid* (Zolst zid a-*zoy* ma-*tern mit*-en *toyt* vee in ma-*ter* zid).

May you go begging from door to door with your descendants for many generations – *Iber di hyzer zolstu zid slepn mit kindskinder oyf dur-durut* (I-ber di hy-*zer zols*-tu zid *slep*-en mi kinds-*kind*-er oyf dur-*dur*-ut).

May you live until one hundred and twenty—with wooden head and glass eyes – *Zolst lebn biz hoondert un tsvantseek yor – mit a heeltsernem kop in glezerne oygn* (Zolst *leb*-en biz *hoond*-ert un *tsvants*-eek yor- mit a *heel*-*tser*-new kop in *glez*-erne *oyg*-en).

May you never be remembered – *Nit gedacht zolstu vern* (Nit ge-*dacht zols*-tu vern).

May you never become old – *Nit derlebn zolstu eltertsu vern* (Nit der-*leb*-en *zols*-tu el-*ter*-tsu vern).

May you never have anything good all your life – *Nit hobn zolstu keyn guts vayl du lebst* (Nit *hob*-en *zols*-tu *key*-en guts *vayl lebst*).

May you never enjoy any goodness in your home – *Nit hobn zolstu keyn guts in* stub (Nit *hob*-en *zols*-tu *key*-en guts in *stub*).

God should visit upon him the best of the Ten Plagues – *Gut zol oyf im onshikn fin di tsen makes di beste (Gut zol oyf in onsh-ikn fin di tsen mak-es di bes-te)*.

All problems I have in my heart, should go to his head – *Ale tsores vos ich hob oyf mayn hartsn, zoln oysgeyn tsu zayn kop (Ale tsor-es vos ich hob oyf may-en harts-en, zoln oysg-eyn tsu zhine kop)*.

On summer days he should mourn, and on wintry nights, he should torture himself - *In di zumerdike teg zol er zitsn shive, un in di vinterdike necht zich raysn ayf di tseyn* (In di zu-*mer*-dike teg zol er *zitsn* shive, un in di vin-*ter*-dike necht zich *rays*-en ayf di *tsey*-en).

It would have been better if a stone had come out of your mother's womb, rather than you – *Beser volt oyf dyn ort a shteyn arayn* (*Be*-ser volt oyf dyn *ort* a *shtey*-en a-*rhine*).

He should have lots of trouble – *Er zol zain ayf tsores* (Er zol *zain* ayf *tsor*-es).

He should have lots of trouble – *Er zol ainemen a miesseh meshuneh* (Er zol ai-*ne*-men a *mies*-eh *mesh*-un-eh).

Wishing someone the worst luck possible

You should have no better luck – *Keyn besern mazel zolstu* (Key-en *bes*-ern *maz*-el *zols*-tu).

May your luck light your way for you like the waning moon at the end of the month - *Dyn mazel zol dir laychtn vee dee levone in sof* (Dyn *maz*-el zol dir *laycht*-en vee dee *lev*-one in *sof*).

Let what I wish on him come true [most, even half, even just 10 percent] – *Zol es im onkumn vos ich vintsh im* [*chotsh a helft, chotsh halb, chotsh a tsent cheyli*] (Zol es im on-*kumn* vos ich *vintsh* im [*chotsh* a *helft, chotsh halb, chotsh* a *tsent chey*-li]).

May you have a long bout of bad luck – *A biter mazel oyf dir* (A bi-*ter maz*-el oyf dir).

His luck should be as bright as a new moon – *Zayn mazel zol im layhtn vee dee levone in sof choydesh* (*zayn maz*-el zol im *layht*-en vee dee *lev*-one in sof choy-desh).

Using a fire wish

May you be consumed by fire – *A fyer zol did farbrenen* (A *fy*-er zol did far-*bren*-en).

May a fire catch hold of you – *A fyer oyf dir* (A *fy*-er oyf dir).

May a fire consume you – *A fyer zucht din* (A *fy*-er *zucht* din). Literally means: A fire is seeking you.

May you be a lamp: hang by day, burn by night and be snuffed out in the morning – *Zolst syn vee a lump: hengen by tog, brenen by nacht in oysgeyn zolstu in der fri* (Zolst syn vee a *lump: heng*-en by tog, *bren*-en by *nacht* in *osy*-geyn *zols*-tu in der fri).

May God see to it that no smoke leaves your chimney for eight consecutive years – *Got zol gebn em zol dir acht yor nun anand nit geyn keyn royn fun koytn* (Got zol *geb*-en em zol dir *acht* yor nun a-*nand* nit *geyn keyn royn* fun *koyt*-en).

A fire should strike you while you are speaking now – *A fyer zol did trefn vee du redst* (A *fy*-er did *tref*-en vee du *redst*).

He should burn up – *A fyer zol im trefn* (A *fy*-er zol im *tref*-en).

Using cats and dogs to hold a grudge

May you speak so eloquently that only a cat will understand you – *Zolst azoy seyn redn az nor di kats zoln dir farshteyn* (Zolst a-*zoy sey*-en *red*-en az nor kats zoln dir *farsht*-eyn).

May you turn into a pancake and be snatched away by the cat – *Vern zol fun dir a blintshik in dee kats zol di chapn* (*Vern* zol fun dir a *blint*-shik in de *kats* zol di *chapn*).

May you turn into a pancake and he into a cat, he should eat you and choke on you; that way we will be rid of both of you – *Vern zol fun did a blintshik in fun is a kats, er sol did oyfesn un mit dir zin dervargn; volt men fun ayn beydn ptur gevorn* (*Vern* zol fun did a *blint*-shik in fun is a *kats*, er sol did oyf-esn un mit dir zin der-*varg*-en *volt* men fun ayn *beyd*-en *ptur* ge-*vorn*).

May your soul enter a cat and may a dog bite it – *Dyn neshome zol arayngeyn in a kats, un a hoont zol er a bis tun* (Dyn ne-*shom*-e zol a-*rhine*-geyn in a *kats* un a *hoont* zol er a bis tun).

Using demons

May your father be possessed by a demon – *A ruech in dayn tatn arayn* (A *ru*-ech in dayn *tat*-en a-*rhine*).

May a demon take your father's father – *A ruech in dayn tatns tatn arayn* (A *ru*-ech in dayn *tat*-ens tatn a-*rhine*).

May your grandfather be possessed by a demon – *A ruech in dayn zeydn arayn* (A *ru*-ech in dayn *zeyd*-en a-*rhine*).

May a demon take your father's son – *A ruech in dayn tatns zun arayn* (A *ru*-ech in dayn *tat*-ens zun a-*rhine*).

May the devil take your thieving father – *A ruech in dayn ganvishn tatn arayn* (A *ru*-ech in dayn gan-*vish*-en *tat*-en a-*rhine*).

6

Yiddish Curses— Short and Sweet

You probably find you get a lot ugly looks if you walk around telling anyone who angers you to "Go fuck yourself"; "Shove it up your ass"; or "Go to hell." You may even get a fist in your mouth. Or get fired from a job.

Don't despair. If you do get that frustrated sometimes, learn a few of these short and sweet Yiddish curses. You can probably even vent your frustration and no one will even know you're cursing.

For example, you can say Put your buttocks on the table (*Toches ahfen tish*) and mean: Put up or shut up (*Too*-ches *Ah*-fin *Tish*)!

Or maybe you prefer, I have him in the bath house (*Ich hob im in bod*) and mean: To hell with him (Ich *hob* im in *bod*)!

Or maybe you'd like, Don't bang on the teakettle (*Hak mir nit kain cheinik*) and mean: Don't bother me (*Hak* meer nit *kayn chy*-nik)!

Yes, there are some roundabout ways to say something in Yiddish, while meaning something very different. You'll also see below that some Yiddish phrases are much more direct for venting your anger.

Do be careful, though. If you're in a Jewish neighborhood, you never know who around you might know Yiddish.

Say the *f* word in Yiddish . . .

Don't fuck with me! – *Bareh nit!* (*Bar*-eh nit)!
Also translates to: Don't fornicate around, or but more mildly can mean don't fool around, or don't annoy or don't bother someone.

Finished fucking? – *Shoyn opgetrent* (*Shoin op*-geh-trent)?
Also translates to: Are you finished screwing around? Or, Have you finished the dirty work? Literally means: Have you finished fornicating?

Go fuck yourself! – *Gai tren zich* (Gay *tren* zich)!

Who are you kidding, who do you think you are screwing around with? –
Vemen barestu (*Vay*-men bar-es-tu)?
Literally means: Who are you screwing?

Use Yiddish to tell someone to go take a sh . . .

Go take a shit! – *Cock zich oys* (*Cock* zich oys)!
Also means: Go take a shit for yourself

Go shit on the ocean! – *Gai cocken ahfen yam* (Gay *cock*-en *ah*-fin *yam*)!
Also can be used to mean: Don't bother me. Or, Get lost

I shit on him. – *Ich cock ahf im* (Ich *cock* ahf im).

Shit on a stick – *Drek oif a shpendel* (Drek oyf a *shpen-del*).
   Also means: As unimportant as dung on a piece of wood.

Get creative using Yiddish to say "kiss my ass"

Kiss my ass! – *Kush mich in toches* (*Kush* mich in *too-ches*)!

Kiss my ass! – *Kush in toches arayn* (*Kush* in *too*-ches a-*rhine*)!

Ass kisser – *Toches lecher* (*Too*-ches *lech*-er).

I've got him by the ass – *Ich hob im in toches* (Ich *hob* im in *too*-ches).
   Also can mean: I have him in my ass.

You ass! – *Chamoyer du einer* (cha-*moy*-er du *eye*-ner)!
   Also can mean: You dope, you idiot!

You should shove it up your ass – *Zolst es shtupin in toches arayn* (Zolst es *shtoop*-en in *too*-ches ar-*ayn*).

Shove it up your ass! – *Shtup es in toches* (*Shtoop* es in *too*-ches)!

Yiddish uses a more friendly sounding way to say "go to hell"

To hell with it – *Zol es brennen* (Zol es *bren*-in).

Oh hell! or Damn it! – *A broch* (Ah *brooch*)!

Go to hell! – *Gai kab enyeh mattereh* (*Gay kab en*-yeh ma-*ter*-eh)!

Go to hell! – *Gai in drerd arayn* (*Gay* in *draird* a-*rhine*)!
Literally means: Go down into the earthly grave.

Go to hell! – *Ich hob dich in drerd* (Ich *hob* dich in *draird*)!

He should go to hell – *A gehenem oif im* (A geh-*hen*-em oyf *im*).

He should go to hell – *Er zol einemen a meeseh meshuneh* (Er *zol ein*-eh-men a *meese*-eh meh-*shun*-eh).

The hell with him! – *Ich hob im in bod* (Ich *hob* im in *bod*)!
Also can be used to say: Forget him! Literally means: I have him in the bath house.

Someone bothering you?
Yiddish can help you vent that

Big deal, so what? – *Groisser gehilleh* (*Groys*-eh geh-*hill*-eh)?

Don't aggravate me! – *Tsap mir nit dos blut* (*Tsap* meer nit *dos blut*)!
Literally means: Don't bleed me!

Don't bother me! – *Drai mir nit kain kop* (*Dray* meer nit *kayn kop*)!
Literally means: Don't twist my head!

Don't bother me! – *Hak mir nit kain cheinik* (*Hak* meer nit *kayn chy*-nik)!
   Literally means: Don't bang on the teakettle!

Don't bother me! – *Chepeh zich nit tsu mir* (*Chep*-eh zich nit *tsu* meer)!
   Literally means: Don't attach yourself to me!

Don't bother me! – *Chepeh zich op fun mir* (*Chep*-eh zich *op* fun meer)!

Don't butt in. Keep your nose out of it. – *Mish zich nisht arayn* (*Mish* zich *nisht* a-*rhine*).

Don't threaten me! - *Strasheh mich nit* (*Stra*-sheh mich nit)!

Get lost! – *Ver farblondjet* (*Vair* far-*blond*-jet)!

Go jump in a lake! – *Nem zich a vaneh* (Nem zich a *van*-eh)!
   Literally means: Go take a bath!

Go bother the bedbugs! – *Gai bareh di vantsen* (*Gay* bar-eh di *vant*-sen)!

Leave me alone! – *Loz mich tzu ru* (*Loz* mich tzu *ru*)!
   Literally means: Let me be in peace!

Leave me alone! - *Chepeh zich op fun mir* (*Chep*-eh zich *op* fun meer)!
   Also means: Get away from me!

So what do you think you can do to me? Nothing. – *Ti mir eppes* (*Tee* mir *ep*-is).

You don't scare me – *Gai strasheh di gens* (*Gay stra* -sheh di *gens*).

> Literally means: Go scare the geese.

I don't give a damn – *Es hart mich vi di vant* (Es *hart* mich vee dee *vant*).

> Literally means: It bothers me like a wall.

You're pissing in the wind – *Gai feifen ahfen yam* (Gay *fife-*en *ah*-fin *yam*).

> Literally means: Go whistle on the wind.

Shut someone up using Yiddish

Put up or shut up! – *Toches ahfen tish* (*Too*-ches *ah*-fin *tish*)!

> Also can be used to mean: Let's conclude this! Or, Come clean, buddy! Literally means: Buttocks on the table.

Shut your mouth! – *Farmach dos moyl* (Far-*mach* dos *moyl*)!

Call them fools, morons and idiots in Yiddish

You moron! – *Chamoyer du ainer* (Cha-*moy*-er du *ain*-er)!

Don't be an idiot! – *Zei nit kain vyzoso* (*Zye* nit kane vi-*zo*-so)!

> Also can mean: Don't be a damn fool! or Don't be a penis!

Don't be a fool! – *Zeit nit kain nar* (*Zye* nit kane *nar*)!

Don't be a fool! *Zeit nit kain goylem* (*Zye* nit kane *go*-lem)!
   Also can mean: Don't be a robot!

Throwing in a few Yiddish body parts

I need it like a hole in the head – *Ich darf es vi a loch in kop* (Ich *darf* es vee a *loch* in *kop*).

Hole in the head – *Loch in kop* (*Loch* in *kop*).

I need it like a wart on my nose – *Ich darf es vi a lung un leber oif der noz* (Ich *darf* es vee *lung* un *leb*-er der *noz*).

Go screw up your head! – *Fardrai zich dem kop* (Far-*dray* zich dem *kop*)!

You should explode! – *Gai plotz* (*Gay plotz*)!
   Also can mean: Go split your guts!

Choke on it! – *Ver dershtikt* (*Vair* der-*shtikt*)!

A few other yiddish shorts for wishing the worst

A horrible end should befall you - *A finsteren sof* (A *fin*-ster-en *sof*).
   Also can mean: May there be a dark ending for you.

A plague on you! – *A finsteren yor* (A *fin*-ster-en *yor*)!
   Literally means: A darkness on you.

A plague on you! - *A choleryeh ahf dir* (A *chol*-er-yeh ayf deer)!

Go drown! – *Ich hob dich in bod* (Ich *hob* dich in *bod*)!
Literally means: I have you in the bath.

Drive yourself crazy! – *Gai fardrai zich dein aigenem kop*
(Gay far-dray zich dine eye-gen-en kop)!

I despise you! - *Ich fief oyf dir* (Ich *fife* oyf deer)!
Literally means: I whistle on you!

An ugly ending to you – *Miesseh meshuneh* (*Meese*-eh ma-*shee*-neh).
Also means: To wish lots of trouble on someone. Literally means: A strange death or a tragic end.

He should have lots of trouble – *Aleh tsores oif zein kop*
(Al-eh *tsor*-es oyf *zine* kop).

A black year! – *A shvartz yor* (A *shvartz* yor)!

7

The Perfect Phrase for the Perfect Putz

I'm sure you know people who just get under your skin. Some because they're just scatterbrains, others because they're dumb, and still others because they are just fools.

Yiddish probably has the perfect word you can use to vent that frustration without letting on that you are frustrated.

Putz, which I use in the title of this chapter, means fool or idiot. It's probably the most well-known Yiddish word for a fool. *Chazzer*, the Yiddish word for a pig, also has found its way into everyday usage. Some of the words you'll find below you've probably heard; most, though, are probably new to you.

Pick the ones that just fit that special someone around you.

Yiddish pet name for that idiot you know

Big idiot – *Groisser putz* (*Groys*-er putz).
  Also means: A big prick, big penis, big fool or big shot.

Butter-fingered – *Shlemiel* (Shleh-*meal*).
  Also can mean: An inept or foolish person, a simpleton, nincompoop or a bungler.

Idiot - *Shmegegi* (Shmeh-*geh*-gee).
Also means: A nothing or a nobody.

Scatterbrain – *Draikop* (*Dray*-kop).
Also means: Someone who goes all out trying to confuse you. Often this refers to a con artist who deliberately is trying to take advantage of you.

Self-made fool – *Shmuck* (*Shmuck*).
Also means: A dickhead, idiot or jerk. Another word for penis. Literally means: Jewel.

Sucker – *Shlumpf* (*Shlumpf*).
Also can mean: A patsy, fall guy or second-rater.

Just the right Yiddish name for that clumsy friend

Clumsy person – *Klutz* (*Klutz*).
Also means: A stupid person or a dolt.

Pitiable person — *Nebach* (*Neb*-ach).

Poor dresser – *Shlump* (*Shloomp*).
Also means: Unstylish or with bad posture. When someone corrects another because his shoulders are drooping, they can say "Don't *shlump!*"

Slob – *Zhlob* (*Zhlob*).
Also means: Someone who is clumsy, uncouth or foolish.

Weakling – *Nebbish* (*Neb*-ish).
Also means: A pitiable person, but not as bad as a *Nebach*.

Naming the incompetent people in your life in Yiddish

Dull-witted – *Poyer* (*Poy*-er).
Also can refer to a peasant, farmer, boor or dullard.

Dreamer – *Luftmensh* (*Luft*-mensh).
Also, can refer to someone who is an unrealistic optimist, builds castles in the air and has no trade or income. You definitely don't want to loan money to a person like this for their next big scheme to make money. Literally means: Air man.

Dumbbell or dunce – *Dumkop* (*Dum*-kop).
Literally means: Dumb head.

Incompentent person – *Loy yitslach* (Loy *yits*-lach).
Also, can refer to someone who has perpetual bad luck.

Incompetent person – *Shlemazel* (Shleh-*mah*-zel)
Also can refer to someone who has perpetual bad luck or misfortunate.

Inexperienced person – *Pisher* (*Pish*-er).
Also used to indicate someone is inexperienced, unseasoned or "wet behind the ears." Or for someone who thinks he's adult enough to handle a task, but really isn't. Another more literal meaning is bed-wetter.

Yiddish name for someone who's just plain annoying

Annoying person – *Nudnik* (*Nood*-nik).
Also used to refer to someone who is a bore, being obnoxious, nagging you, or generally being a nuisance.

Ass kisser – *Toches-lecker* (*Too*-ches *leck*-er).
Also can refer to a brown-noser or someone who will do anything to gain favor. Literally means: Buttock-licker.

Big good-for-nothing – *Groisser gornisht* (*Groys*-er gornisht).

Braggart – *Shvitzer* (*Shvitz*-er).
Literally means: Someone who sweats.

Complainer – *Kvetcher* (*Kvetch*-er).
Also can refer to someone who is a whiner. Nothing is ever good enough for them. Rodney Dangerfield was known as the king of the *kvetchers*. *Kvetch* in Yiddish is to squeeze.

Gossip – *Yenta* (*Yen*-teh).
Also can refer to someone who is a busybody, talkative woman or blabbermouth.

Impolite person – *Bulvan* (*Bul*-van).
Also means: A rude or ill-mannered person.

Informer – *Mosser* (*Moo*-ser).

Lazy man – *Foiler* (Foy-ler).

Lecherous old man – *Alter kucker* (Al-ter *kuck*-er).
Also means: Old fogy. Literally means: An old defecator.

Liar – *Ligner* (*Lig*-ner).

Panhandler – *Shnorrer* (*Shnor*-er).
Also can refer to someone who is a beggar, moocher or

freeloader. *Shnorrers* make a career of panhandling and
think they are doing others a favor by allowing them to do
a *mitzvah* (good deed) though donating to the needy.

Pig – *Chazzer* (*Chaz*-er).
Also can refer to someone who is greedy, eats too much or
takes more than his share.

Smelly person – *Shtinker* (*Shtink*-er).
Also can refer to someone who behaves offensively.

Sponger – *Shlepper* (*Shlep*-per).
Also can refer to someone who always tags along or a jerk.

Giving bastards a Yiddish nickname

Bastard – *Mamzer* (Mamz-er).
Also someone who is a nasty, unworthy person.

Bimbo – *Tzatzkeh* (*Tzatz*-keh).
Also can refer to someone who is a mistress, sexually
attractive girl or an overdressed woman. Another meaning
can be a toy, ornament or expensive plaything.

Crazy bastard – *Meshugener mamzer* (Meh-*shu*-gen-er
mamz-er).
Its origins are from the Hebrew word *meshugga* (meh-*shu*-
ga) for crazy, and *mamzer* for bastard.

Drunkard – *Shikker* (*Shik*-er).
Also means: To be drunk.

Piece of shit – *Shtik drek* (*Shtick* drek).

Pimp – *Yentzer* (*Yents*-er).
Also refers to someone who will screw you in a nonsexual way.

Shit head – *Kucker* (*Kuck*-er).

Thief – *Gonif* (*Gon*-if).
Also can be used to refer to someone who is a swindler, crook, burglar or racketeer.

Trashy – *Drek* (*Drek*).
Also can be used to refer to someone who is cheap, trashy, shoddy, worthless or useless.

8
Yiddish Body Blows

When you're just about ready to take a strike at someone, but don't really want to hurt your hand, you may want to use some Yiddish curses instead. Just to give you an idea of how effective these verbal body blows can be in relieving some tension, let's listen in on a dinner conversation between Hannah and Sarah after Hannah's boyfriend dumped her. . . .

SARAH: So, *nu*? What happened?

HANNAH: That *shmuck* decided things were getting too serious for him and thought it's time for us to cool it for a while.

SARAH: What a *putz*! You've been seeing each other for two years now, right?

HANNAH: Yes. "*Got zol gebn, er zol hobn altsding vos zayn harts glist, nor er zol zayn geleymt oyf ale ayvers un nit kenen rirn mit der tsung,*" meaning "God should bestow him with everything his heart desires, but he should be a quadriplegic and not be able to use his tongue." (*Got* zol *beb*-en er zol *hob*-n alts-*ding* vos *zayn harts glist,* nor er zol *zayn* ge-*leymt* oyf ale ay-vers un nit *ken*-en rirn mit der *tsung.*)

SARAH: I can understand your anger, but might that be a bit harsh? Maybe this would fit better. "*Ale tseyn zoln dir aroysfaln, nor eyner zol dir blaybn—oyf tsonveytik.*" That means, "May all your teeth fall out, except one to give you a toothache." (*Al*-e *tsey*-en zoln dir a-*roys*-falen, nor *eyn*-er zol dir *blayb*-en—oyf tson-*vey*-tik.)

HANNAH: Nope, that doesn't work for me. A toothache is just not enough *tsores.* You might find this more acceptable. "*Zoln dir vaksn burekes fun pupik, in zolst pishn mit borsht.*" Meaning, "May a red beet grow out of your belly button, and may you pee borsht." (*Zoln* dir *vaks*-en bu-*rek*-es fun *pup*-ik in *zolst pish*-en mit *borsht.*)

SARAH: Yuck! Borsht is one of my grandmother's favorite cold soups. Doesn't sound like much of a punishment, but it could be embarrassing, especially if it leaks out at the most inopportune moments.

HANNAH: Yeah. Like in front of his boss. But maybe you're right. I've got to find something that would be more painful, but not quite as bad as wishing he become quadriplegic. Hmm . . . how about this? "*Nezunt un shtark zolstu zayn vee ayzn, zolst zid nit kenen,*" which means, "May you be healthy and tough as iron, so much so that you cannot bend over." (Ne-*zunt* un *shtark zols*-tu zayn vee *ayz*-en *zolst* zid nit *ken*-en.)

SARAH: I think you've got it. Sounds like just the right touch. But, I know this is not the first time you too have split for a while.

HANNAH: Nope, this is the third time.

SARAH: Are you sure this is it? Do you think you might get back together.

HANNAH: Not this time. I'm a strong believer in my grandmother's Yiddish proverb *"Ain mol a saichel, dos tsvaliteh mol chain, dem dritten mol git men in di tsain,"* which means, "The first time it's smart, the second time it's cute, the third time you get a sock in the teeth." (Ain mol a sai-*chel* dos tsva-*lit*-eh mol *chain*, dem *drit*-ten mol git men in di *tsain*.) That sock in the teeth is the only thing he'll get from me, if he tries to come back. It's time for me to move on.

Yiddish curses can get pretty gross in what can be wished on others. I've grouped some top choices below by parts of the body.

Taking Yiddish blows to the head, teeth, neck and tongue

May a disease enter his gums – *A krenk zol im arayn in di yosles* (A *krenk* zolim a-*rhine* in dee *yos*-lis).

All his teeth should fall out except one to make him suffer – *Ale tseyn zoln bay im aroysfalen, not eyner zol im blay-ben oyf tsonveytung* – (Ale *tseyn zoln bay* im a-*roys*-fal-en not *eyn*-er zol in *blayb*-en ofy tson-*veyt*-ung).

May you be in mourning in summer days and suffer from a toothache on winter nights – *In dee zumerdike tig zolstu zitsen shiveh un in dee vinterdike necht zolstu zid rayst oyf dee seyn* (In dee zu-*mer*-di-ke tig *zols*-tu *zits*-en *shi*-veh un in dee vin-*ter*-di-ke *nect zols*-tu zid *rayst* oyf dee *seyn*).

Those who can't bite should not show their teeth. – *Az men ken nit beissen, zol men nit veizen di tsain* (Az men ken nit *beis*-en zol men nit *veiz*-en di *tsain*).

May a bone remain stuck in your throat – *A beyn zol dir in haldz blayben shtekn* (A *beyn* zol dir in *haldz blayb*-en *shtek*-en).

A rope around your neck – *A shtrek dir oyfn haldz* (A *shtrek* dir oyf-en *haldz*).

He should grow a wooden tongue – *A hiltsener tsung zol er bakumn* (A hil-*tsen*-er zol er ba-*kumn*).

He should grow like an onion with his head in the ground – *Er zol vaksen vi a tsibeleh, mit dem kop in drerd* (Er zol *vak*-es-en a *tsib*-el-eh, mit dem *kop* in *drerd*).

May a cannon ball split your skull – *A harmat zol dayn kop tseshmetern* (A *harm*-at zol *dayn kop* tsesh-*met*-ern).

May a soft balcony fall on your head – *A vecher balkon dir in kop* (A *vech*-er *bal*-kon dir in *kop*).

May a wheel run over your skull – *A rud zol dir ariber iber dee gehirn* (A *rud* zol dir a-*rib*-er i-*ber* dee ge-*hirn*).

Go break you own head! – *Shlog zich kog in vant!* (*Shlog* zich *kog* in *vant*)!

Throw salt in his eyes, pepper in his nose – *Zalts im in di oygen, feffer im in di noz* (*Zalts* im in di *oyg*-en, *fef*-er im in di *noz*).

Doing in the bones using Yiddish body blows

I hope to see you on one leg and may you see me with one eye – *Id zol did zen oyf eyn foos un du mid-mit eyn oyg* (Id zol did *zen* oyf eyn *fus* un du *mid*—mit eyn *oyg*).

He should break a leg – *Zol er tzebrechne a fus* (Zol er tze-*brech*-en a *foos*).

Go break a leg! – Gai tsebrech a fus (*Gay* tse-*brech* a foos)!

May your legs be lopped from under you – *Dee fim zoln dir untergehakt vern* (Dee fim *zoln* dir un-ter-*gehakt vern*).

May you break your arms and your legs – *Oysbrechen zolstu dee hent mit dee fus* (Oys-*brech*-en *zols*-tu dee *hent* mit dee *foos*).

May your arms and hands be paralyzed – *Opkenumen zoln dir dee hent vern* (Op-*ken*-u-men zoln dir dee *hent vern*).

May your bones rot in hell – *Dayne beyner zoln foylen in gihnum* (Dayne *beyn*-er zoln *foyl*-en in gih-*num*).

May cholera rot your bones – *A cholere dir in dee beyner* (A *chol*-er-e dir in dee *beyn*-er).

May you break all your bones – *Tseboyechen zolstu ruk-un-lend* (Tse-*boy*-ech-en *zols*-tu *ruk*-un-*lend*).
Literally means: May you break your back and your sides.

He who throws stones on another gets them back on his own bones – *Ver es varft oil yenem shteyner krigt tsurik in di aigneh bainer* (Ver es *varft* oil *yen*-em *shteyn*-er krigt *tsur*-ik in di *aig*-neh *bain*-er).

Stones on his bones – *Shteyner ayf zayne bainer* (*Shteyn*-er ayf *zayne bain*-er).

Going inside the body with Yiddish body blows

Onions should grow on your navel – *Zol dir vaksn tzibbeles fun pupik* (Zol dir *vax*-en *tzib*-eh-les fun *poop*-ik).

May your intestines be pulled out of your belly and wound around your neck – *Aroysshlepn zol men dir dee kishkes fun boyd un arumviklen zee ebern haldz* (A-*roys*-shlepen zol men dir dee *keesh*-kes fun *boyd* un a-*rum*-viklen zee e-*bern haldz*).

May your liver come out through your nose piece by piece – *Dee leber zol dir shteklechvayz doord der noz aroysfleen* (Dee *leb*-er dir shtek-*lech*-vayz doord der noz a-*roys*-fleen).

May your guts come out – *Dee kishkes zoln dir aroym* (Dee *keesh*-kes zoln dir a-*roym*).

Your stomach will rumble so badly, you'll think it was a Purim noisemaker – *Es zol dir dunern in boych, vestu meyen az s'iz a homon klaper* (Es zol dir *dun*-ern in *boych*, *ves*-tu *mey*-en az s'iz a *hom*-on *klap*-er).

For those not familiar with the holiday of Purim, as part of the celebration various kinds of noisemakers are used to drown out the name of the enemy of the Jews—Haman—as the story of Esther is told during the reading of the Megillah, which is the book of Esther.

You should only get a stomach cramp – *Zol dich chappen beim boych* (Zol dich *chap*-in byme *boych*).

A cramp in your stomach – *A kramp dir in boyd* (A *kramp* dir in *boyd*).

You should get a stomach cramp – *Zol dir grihmen in boych* (Zol dir *grih*-men in *boych*).

A stabbing pain in your stomach – *A shnaydenish dir in boyd* (A *shnay*-de-nish dir in *boyd*).

When the stomach is empty, so is the brain – *Az der mogen iz laidik iz der moi'ech oich laidik* (Az der *mog*-en iz *laid*-ik iz der *moi'*ech *oich laid*-ik).

He should crap blood and pus – *Er zol kakn mit blit un mit ayter.* (Er zol *kak*-en mit *blit* un mit *ayt*-er).

You should choke on it – *Der shtikt zolst du veren* (Der *shtikt* zolst du *ver*-en).

You can vomit from this – *Me ken brechen fun dem* (Me ken *brech*-en fun dem).

May a boil grow on your belly-button – *S'zol dir vaksn a geshver oyfn pupik* (S'zol dir *vaks*-en a *gesh*-ver oyf-en *poo*-pik).

May a fire burn in your guts – *A brand dir in dee kishkes* (A *brand* dir in dee *keesh*-kes).

May a fire burn in your stomach – *A fyer dir in boyd* (A *fy*-er dir in *boyd*).

May a fire inflame your liver – *A fyer in doyn leber* (A *fy*-er in *doyn leb*-er).

Body-wide Yiddish body blows

You should swell up like a mountain – *Zolst geshvolln veren vi a barg* (Zolst geh-*shvol*-en *ver*-en vi a *barg*).

A boil is fine as long as it's under someone else's arm – *A geshvir iz a gutch zach bei yenem unhern orem* (A *gesh*-vir iz a *gutch* zach bei *yen*-em un-*hern* o-*rem*).

May a thunder shake your body – *A duner dir in dee zaytn arayn* (A *dun*-er dir in dee *zayt*-en a-*rhine*).

May you break down and collapse – *Ayngebrochn zolstu vern* (Aynge-*broch*-en *zols*-tu vern).

A cramp in his body [in his stomach, in his guts, in his bowels, in his fingers and toes] – *A kramp im in layb* [*in boyach, in di kishkes, in di gederem, in di finger*] (A *kramp* in *layb* [in *boy*-ach, in di *keesh*-kes, in di *ged*-er-em, in di *fing*-er].

Leeches should drink him dry – *Trinkn zoln im piavkes* (*Trink*-en zoln im *piav*-kes).

He should be transformed into a chandelier: to hang by day and to burn by night – *Migulgl zol er vern in a henglayhter: bay tog zol er hengn, un bay nacht zol er brenen* (Mi-*gul*-gel zol er *vern* in a heng-*layht*-er: bay tog zol er *heng*-en, un bay *nacht* zol er *bren*-en).

It's useless; it'll help like bloodletting on a dead body – *Es vet helfn vi a toitn bahnekes* (Es vet *helf*-en vee a *toyt*-en *bahn*-kis).

9

Wishing Someone Ill— Yiddish-Style

Many Yiddish insults involve the creative use of body parts and body functions to wish that someone get sick. It was rare that someone would directly wish an illness on someone else; instead, they would say something nice and sock it to them at the end, such as by using this favorite: "I hope I can come to you on joyous occasions and that you will come to me on crutches" – *Id tsu dir oyf simchut, du tsu mir oyf kuliem* (Id tsu dir oyf sim-*chut*, du tsu mir oy ku-*li*-em). Now why that person should be on crutches . . . They wouldn't bother to mention that.

Or they would wish something so outrageous, "You should swell up like a mountain – *Zolst geshvollen veren vi a barg* (Zolst geh-*shvol*-en *ver*-en vi a *barg*), which of course could never happen, but leaves a very visual impression of how high their anger has built.

Or it could be something that was an unthinkable wish. "She should have stones and not children" – *Shteyner zol zi hoben, nit kayn kinder* (*Shtey*-ner zol zi *hob*-en, nit *kayn kin*-der).

Most of these curses were wishes for longtime illnesses or suffering using various body parts or body malfunctions. Frequent doctors' visits or eating troubles were another common theme. Here are some favorites grouped by their themes.

Wishing frequent doctor visits

He should give it all away to doctors – *Oyf doktoyrim zol er dos avekgebn* (Oyf *dok*-toy-rim zol er dos a-*vek*-geb-en).

If anyone writes you, they should write you doctors' prescriptions – Shraybn zol men dir retseptn (*Shrayb*-en zol men dir re-*tsept*-en).

May doctors know you well and vice versa – *Doktoyrim zoln vesen fun dir un di fun doktoyrim* (*Dok*-toy-rim zoln *ves*-en fun dir un di fun *dok*-toy-rim).

Wishing food troubles

He should drink too much castor oil – *Azoy fil ritzinoyl zol er oystrinkn* (A-*zoy* fil rit-*zin*-oyl zol er oy-*strink*-en).

He should get so sick as to cough up his mother's milk – *Oyskrinkn zol er dus mame's milach* (Oy-*strink*-en zol er dus *ma*-me's *mil*-ach).

From overeating one suffers more than from not eating enough – *Fun iberessn cholyet men mer vi fun nit deressn* (Fun i-*ber*-es-sen *chol*-yet men mer vi fun nit *der*-es-sen).

May you choke on a fish dumpling – *A feshkneydh zol zid dir shtelnin haldz* (A fesh-*kneyd*-eh zol zid dir *shtel*-nin *haldz*).

Wishing stomach troubles

May you have a revolution in your stomach – *S'zol dir dreyn in boyd* (S'*zol* dir *drey*-en in *boyd*).

May you have terrible stabbing pains in your bowels – *S'zol dir shnaydn bay di kishkes* (S'zol dir *shnayd*-en bay di *keesh*-kes).

May you run to the toilet every three minutes or every three months – *Loyn zolstu in bet-chakis iede dray minut oder iede dray chadoshim* (*Loyn zols*-tu in bet-*chak*-is i-ed-e *dray min*-ut o-*der* i-ed-e *dray cha*-do-shim).

May your guts freeze so hard that only hellfire will be able to thaw them – *Zoln dayn kishkes farfrayrn vern oyf azoy fil, az nor der fyer fun gehnum zol zey kenen tseshmeltsn* (Zoln *dayn kish*-kes far-*frayr*-en vern oyf a-*zoy* fil, az nor der *fy*-er fun *geh*-num zol zey *ken*-en tsesh-*melt*-sen).

Causing yourself illness

He talks himself into sickness – *Er redt zich eyn a krenk* (Er *redt* zich eyn a *krenk*).

If you invest in a fever, you will realize a disease – *Az me laight arayn kadoches, nemt men aroyz a krenik* (Az me *laight* a-*rhine* ka-*doch*-es, nemt men a-*royz* a *kren*-ik).

If you keep on talking, you will end up saying what you didn't intend to say – *Az me redt, derredt men zich* (Az me *redt*, *der*-redt men zich).

Worms eat you up when dead and worries eat you up alive – *Verem essn toiterhayt un deiges lebedikerhayt* (Ve-*rem* es-sen toi-*ter*-hayt un *dei*-ges le-*bed*-i-ker-*hayt*).

If you tell a lie may you lie ill – *Oyb du zogst lign zolstu krenk lign* (Oyb du *zogst* li-*gen* zols-tu *krenk* li-*gen*).

Go drive yourself crazy – *Gai fardrai zich deyn kop* (*Gay far*-dray zich *deyn kop*).

Go bang your head against the wall! – *Gai klop zich kop in vant* (*Gay klop* zich *kop* in *vant*)!

Hoping someone chokes

May you choke on your next bite on your food – *Dershtikt zolstu vern mit bisn* (Der-*shtikt* zols-tu vern mit *bis*-en).

May you choke on your next juicy morsel – *Dershtikt zolstu dir mit dem fatn bisn* (Der-*shtikt* zols-tu dir mit dem *fat*-en *bis*-en).

May you enjoy your wedding breakfast and choke on your last bite – *Zolst hobn hano'ie fun dayn chuneh-seudeh un zid dervargn mit letstn bisn* (*Zolst hob*-en ha-*no*'ie fun *dayn chun*-eh *seu*-deh un zid der-*varg*-en mit *letst*-en *bis*-en).

Wishing general body-wide illnesses

May you own ten ships full of gold and may you spend it all on your illnesses – *Tsen shifn mit gold zolstu farmogn in dos gantse gelt zolstu farkrenkn* (Tsen *shif*-en mit gold *zols*-tu far-*mog*-en in do *gant*-se *gelt zols*-tu far-*kenk*-en).

May God give you a large cancer as well as a small cancer – and then you will have a nice outfit - *Got zol dir gebn a rak mit a rekele—vestu hobn a gantsn kostium* (Got zol dir *geb*-en a *rak* mit a *rek*-e-le—*ves*-tu *gants*-en *kos*-ti-um).
  In Yiddish this is a pun. The Yiddish word *rak* is both a term for cancer and a term for jacket.

May sickness drain all you have and may you pawn your wife's skirt – *Oyskrenkn zolstu alts vos du farmogst un farzetsn der vaybs spodnitse* (Oys-*krenk*-en *zols*-tu alts vos du far-*mogst* un far-*zets*-en der *vayb*-es spod-*nit*-se).

A fever should toss you (in bed) a foot high each time – *Varfn zol did eylenvayz* (Var-*fen* zol did ey-*len*-wayz).

God should visit upon him the best of the Ten Plagues – *Got zol oyf im onshikn fin di tsen makes di beste* (*Got* zol oyf im on-*shik*-en fun di *tsen mak*-es di *bes*-te).

Venereal disease should consume his body – *Fransn zol esn zayn layb* (*Frans*-en zol esn *zayn layb*).

A plague on you – *A choleryeh oyf dir* (A *chol*-er-yeh ayf deer).

A plague should befall you – *A magaifeh zol dich trefen* (A ma-*gay*-feh *zol* dich *tref*-en).

Better that you should live and suffer – *Zolst beser lebn . . . un mutshen zid* (*Zolst bes*-er *leb*-en . . . un mut-*shen* zid).

May suffering consume you – *Oysgerisn zolstu vern* (Oys-ger-isn zols-tu vern).

May you explode from pleasure – *Platsn zolstu—fun naches* (*Plats*-en zols-tu—fun *nach*-es).

May you fall and never rise up – *Faln zolstu nit oyfshteyn* (*Fal*-en zols-tu ni oyf-*shteyn*).

May you feel pricks, bites, aching bones and sores all over your body – *S'zol did onchapn a shtechenish un a brechenish, a raysenish un a baysenish* (S'zol did on-*chap*-en a *shtech*-en-ish un a *brech*-en-ish, a *ryas*-en-ish una *bays*-en-ish).

May an epidemic strike you – *A mageyfe zol oyf dir kumen* (A ma-*geyf*-e zol oyf dir *kum*-en).

May syphilis consume your flesh – *Frantsn zoln esn dayn dayb* (*Frants*-en zoln esn *dayn dayb*).

May you be consumed by syphilis and may your nose drop off – *Frantsn zoln dir oyf esn un din noz zol dir arop-faln* (*Frants*-en zoln dir oyf esn un din *noz* zol dir a-*rop*-fal-en).

10
Yiddish Mind Games

People loved to use Yiddish to play all kinds of mind games. In some cases, rather than wish someone a physical illness, they preferred to wish they go crazy, to get them out of their way—using phrases like "*A meshugener zol men oyshrabn, un im arayn shrabn.*" – "They should free a madman, and lock him up." (A me-*shug*-en-er zol men oy-*shrab*-en, un im a-*rhine shrab*-en.)

Other times, words of Yiddish wisdom expressed things a mother thought everyone should ponder. "*A kluger vaist vos er zogt, a nar zogt vos er vaist.*" – "A wise man knows what he says, a fool says what he knows." (A *klug*-er vaist vos er *zogt*, a *nar* zogt vos er *vaist.*)

But even better . . . for those who have been fool enough to piss off their rabbi (religious leader), "*Az men krigt zich mitn rov, muz men sholem zeyn mitn shainker.*" "If you're at odds with your rabbi, make peace with your bartender." (Az men *krigt* zich *mit*-en rov, muz men *shol*-en zyen *mit*-en *shaink*-er.)

Here are some variations on how to wish someone crazy, talk about fools, find fools talking about themselves or just some words of Yiddish wisdom for the mind:

Wishing someone crazy

May you go crazy and run around the streets – *Meshugeh zolstu vern un orumloyfn iber dee gasn* (Me-*shug*-eh *zols*-tu vern un o-*rum*-loyf-en i-ber dee *gas*-en).

Go drive yourself crazy – *Fardray zich dayn aygenem kop* (Far-*dray* zich *dayn* ay-*gen*-em).

Go mix yourself up, not me – *Gai fardray zich dayn aigenem kop* (*Gay* far-*dray* zich *dayn* ay-*gen*-em).

May I not lose anything more than your head – *Mer vi dayn kop zol id nit onvern* (Mer vi *dayn kop* zol id nit on-*vern*).

May illness strike your brain – *A chvarobe dir in dee gehern* (A *chvar*-ob-e dir in dee ge-*her*-en).

You're nuts – *Bist meshugeh* (Bist me-*shug*-eh).

You're nuts – *Bist tsedrayt* (Bist tse-*drayt*).

Are you crazy – *Tsi bistu meshugeh* (Tsi-*bis*-tu me-*shug*-eh)?

Talking about fools . . . or fools talking

When the head is a fool, the whole body can go to hell – *Az der kop iz a nar, ligt der gantser guf in der erd* (Az der *kop* iz a *nar, ligt* der *gants*-er guf in der *erd*).

He who keeps quiet is half a fool; he who talks is a complete fool – *Az me shvaygt iz men a halber nar; az me redt iz men a gantser nar* (Az me *shvagt* iz men a *halb*-er nar; az me *redt* iz men a *gants*-er nar).

If you repeat often enough that you're right, you will discover you are wrong – *Az men chazert tsu fil iber vi grecht men iz, vert men umgerecht* (Az men *chaz*-ert tsu fil i-ber vi *grecht* men iz, vert men um-*ger*-echt).

If you're a child at twenty, you're an ass at twenty-one – *Az men iz biz tsvantsik yor a kind, iz men tsu ayn-un-tsvantsik a behaymeh* (Az men iz biz *tsvant*-sik yor a *kind*, iz men tsu ayn un *tsvant*-sik a be-*hay*-meh).

Passing on one's troubles

All the troubles [which weigh down my heart] should fall on your head – *Ale tsores [vos id hob oyf mayn hartn] zoln oysgeyn tsu dayn kop* (Ale *tsor*-es [vos id *hob* oyf *mayn hart*-en] zoln osy-*gey*-en tsu *dayn kop*).

May all the possible bad dreams stuff your head – *Ale beyze chlumut tsu dayn kop* (Ale *beyz*-e *chlum*-ut tsu *dayn kop*).

May trouble come upon your head – *A brod tsu dayn kop* (A *brod* tsu *dayn kop*).

May you be struck dumb forever – *Antshvign zolstu vern oyf eybik* (Ant-*shvig*-en *zols*-tu vern oyf ey-*bik*).

Passing on words of wisdom

One lie is a lie, two are lies, but three is politics – *Ayner iz a ligen, tsvai iz ligens, dray iz politik.* (Ay-*ner* iz a *lig*-en, *tsvai* iz *lig*-ens, *dray* iz pol-*it*-ik).

When a mother shouts at her child, "Bastard," you can believe her – *Az di muter shrayt oyfen kind, "Mamzer," meg men ir gloiben* (Az di mu-*ter shrayt* oyf-en *kind,* "*mam*-zer," meg men ir *gloib*-en).

He who lives with the devil, becomes a devil - *Az me lebt mit a tayvel, vert men a tayvel.* (Az me *lebt* mit a *tayv*-el, vert men a *tayv*-el).

Give a pig a chair, he'll want to get on the table – *Az me lozt a chazzer aruf af'n bank, viler af'n tish* (Az me *lozt* a *chazz*-er a-ruf af'n *bank,* vil-er af'n *tish*).

If you lie down with the dogs, you get up with the fleas – *Az me shloft mit hint, shtayt men oyf mit flay* (Az me *shloft* mit *hint, shtayt* men oyf mit *flay*).

Better a crooked foot than a crooked mind – *Beser a krumer fus ayder a krumer kop* (*Bes*-er a *krum*-er fus ay-*der* a *krum*-er *kop*).

Better to do nothing than to make something into nothing – *Beser dos kind zol vaynen ayder der foter* (*Bes*-er dos kind *zol vayn*-en ay-*der* der *fot*-er).

Run away from an insult but don't chase after honor – *Far umkoved antloyf, ober yog zich nit noch koved* (*Far* um-kov-ed ant-*loyf,* o-ber *yog* zich nit *noch* ko-*ved*).

With a good guest, you are happy when he arrives; with a bad one, when he leaves – *Mit a gutn gast frayt men zich ven er kumt arayn; mit a shlechtn gast, ven er gayt avek* (Mit gu-*ten* gas *frayt* men zich ven er *kumt* a-*rhine*; mit a *shlecht*-en gast, ven er *gayt* a-*vek*).

If you want to please everybody, you'll die before your time – *Vest vellen zich oysfaynen far layt, vestu shtarbn far der tsayt* (*Vest vell*-en zich oys-*fay*-nen far *layt, ves*-tu *shtarb*-en far der *tsayt*).

As you make your bed, so will you sleep in it – *Vi me bet zich oys, azoy darf men shlofn.* (Vi me bet *zich* oys, a-*zoy* darf men *shlof*-en).

11

Money
Madness
in Yiddish

Yiddish was the primary language of money/business among Jews. Sometimes Yiddish money curses wished someone everything financially, but with a backhanded curse of unending illness. For example:

> A hundred houses shall he have, in every house a hundred rooms and in every room twenty beds, and a delirious fever should drive him from bed to bed – *Hindert hayzer zol er hobn, in yeder hoyz a hindert tsimern, in yeder tsimer tsvonsik betn un kaduches zol im varfn fin eyn bet in der tsveyter* (*Hind*-ert hay-zer zol er *hob*-en, in *yed*-er *hoyz* a *hind*-ert *tsim*-ern in *yed*-er *tsim*-er *tsvon*-sik *bet*-en un ka-*duch*-es zol im *varf*-en fin eyn bet in der *tsveyt*-er).

or

> Ten ships of gold should be his and the money should only make him sick – *Tsen shifn mit gold zol er farmorgn, un dos gantse gelt zol er farkrenkn* (*Tsen shif*-en mit gold zol er far-*morg*-en un does *gant*-se getl zol er far-*krenk*-en).

Another common wish was one for great business success, but no way to use it:

He should see everything, but have no reason [with what] to buy it – *Er zol altsting zen, un nit hobn farvos [mit vos] tsu koyfn (Er zol als-ting zen, un nit hob-en far-vos [mit vos] tsu koyf-en).*

He should have a large store: whatever people ask for he shouldn't have, and what he does have shouldn't be requested—*A groys gesheft zol er hobn mit shroyre: vus er hot, zol men bay im nit fregn, un vos men fregt zol er nisht hobn* (A groys ge-*sheft* zol er *hob*-en mit *shroy*-re: vu ser hot, zol men bay im nit *freg*-en, un vos men *fregt* zol er *nisht hob*-en).

Money wisdoms centered around friends or enemies and money, and being rich or the problems of being rich. Often, sayings show the love/hate relationship Jews have with money. Here are some examples of money wisdom:

Friends or enemies—and your money

A friend you can get for nothing; an enemy has to be bought – *A freint bekamt men umzist; a soineh muz men zich koifn* (A *freint bek*-amt men um-*zist*; a *soi*-neh muz men zich *koif*-en).

A friend you have to buy; enemies you get for nothing – *A freint darf men zich koifn; sonem kright men umzist* (A *freint* darf men zich *koif*-en; *son*-em *kright* men um-*zist*).

The poor man's enemies are few, the rich man's friends are even fewer – *Der oreman hot vainik eint, der reicher hot vainiker freint* (Der *ore*-man hot *vain*-ik, der *reich*-er hot *vain*-ik-er *freint*).

Rich men and their money

If you have money, you are wise and good-looking and can sing well too – *Az me hot gelt, iz men klug un shain un men ken gut zingn (Az me hot gelt, iz men* klug *un* shain *un men* ken *gut* zing-*en).*

If one steals a lot of eggs, one can also become rich – *Az men ganvet a sach ayer, ken men oich verren a nogid.* (Az men *gan*-vet a *sach* ay-er, *ken* men *oich ver*-ren a *nog*-id).

If you have the money, you have the "say." – *Az men hot di matbayeh, hot men di dayeh* (Az men hot di mat-*bay*-eh, hot men di *day*-eh).

Who is smart? He whose fortune follows him. - *Der iz klug? Vos zeyn mazel gayt im noch* (Der iz *klug?* Vos zeyn *maz*-el *gayt* im *noch.)*

Fortune makes you smart, because fortune makes you rich – *Der mazel macht klug, veil der mazel macht reich* (Der *maz*-el macht *klug,* veil der *maz*-el macht *reich*).

Money goes to money – *Gelt gayt tsu gelt* (Gelt *gayt* tsu gelt).

You cannot pay a debt with a noble pedigree –*Mit zechus oves batsolt men nit kayn choyves* (Mit *zach*-us oves *bat*-solt men nit *kayn choy*-ves).

When does a wealthy man go hungry? When the doctor orders him! – *Ven hungert a nogid? Ven der doktor hayst im!* (Ven *hung*-ert a *nog*-d? Ven der *dokt*-or *hayst* im!)

May you become so rich that your widow's husband should never have any worries about his livelihood – *Zolst vern azoy rayd almo'nes man zol zid keyn mol nit zorgen vegn perno'se* (Zolst vern a-*zoy rayd* almo'nes man zol zid *keyn* mol nit *zorg-*en *veg-*en).

May you spend all your money on doctors – *Farkrenk dos oyf dayn guf* (Far-*krenk* dos oyf *dayn* guf).
Literally means: May you spend all your money on your body.

Money wisdoms

From fortune to misfortune is a short step; from misfortune to fortune is a long way – *Fun glik tsum umglik iz a shpan; fun umglik tsum glik iz a shtik veg* (Fun *glik* tsum um-*glik* iz a *shpan*; fun um-*glik* iz a *shtik* veg).

When you grease the palm, everything goes easy – *Az me shmirt, fort men* (Az me *shmirt*, fort men).

If you don't save the penny, you'll not have the dollar – *Az me shport nit dem groshn, hot men nit dem rubel* (Az me *shport* nit dem *grosh-*en, hot men nit dem *rub-*el).

From litigation you can never recover your loss – *Az me tut zich lodn, kumt men sey vi nit tsum shodn* (Az me tut zich *lod-*en, kumt men sey vi nit tsum *shod-*en).

When you sow money, you reap fools – *Az me zayt gelt, vaksn naronim* (Az me *zayt* gelt, *vaks-*en na-*ron-*im).

So it goes in this world: one has the purse the other has the money – *Azoy gayt ayf der velt: ayner hot di beytel, der tsvayter hot di gelt* (A-*zoy gayt* ayf der velt: *ayn*-er hot di *beyt*-el der *tsvayt*-er hot di *gelt*).

Life is the biggest bargain—we get it for nothing – *Der lebn iz di gresteh metsi'eh—me wrigt es umzist* (Der *leb*-en iz di *grest*-eh met-si'eh—me *wrigt* es um-*zist*).

The heaviest burden is an empty pocket – *Der shversteh ol iz a laydikeh kesheneh* (Der *shverst*-eh ol iz a *layd*-ik-eh *kesh*-en-eh).

For the smallest favor you become a debtor – *Far der klenster toyveh vert men a ba'al-choyv* (Far der *klenst*-er *toyv*-eh vert men a ba'al-*choyv*).

Lost years are worse than lost dollars – *Farloreneh yoren iz erger vi farloreneh gelt* (Far-*lor*-en-eh *yor*-en iz *erg*-er vi far-*lor*-en-eh gelt).

Love/hate relationship with money

Money buys everything except brains – *Far gelt bakumt men alts, nor kain saychel nit* (Far gelt *bak*-umt men alts, nor *kain say*-chel nit).

Rich men are often lean and poor men are fat – *Faran dareh gvirim un feteh oremeleyt* (*Far*-an *dar*-eh ge-*vir*-im un *fet*-eh o-*rem*-el-eyt).

Money causes conceit and conceit leads to sin – *Gelt brengt tsu ga'aveh un ga'aveh tsu zind* (Gelt *brengt* tsu ga'a-veh un ga'a-vch tsu zind).

Money lost, nothing lost; courage lost, everything lost –
Gelt farloren, gor nit farloren; mut farloren, alts farloren
(Gelt far-*lor*-en, gor nit far-*lor*-en; mut far-*lor*-en, alts far-
lor-en).

God helps the poor man; he protects him from expensive
sins – *Got helft dem oreman: er farhit im fun tey'ereh
avayres* (*Got* helft dem o-*re*-man: er *far*-hit im fun tey'er-eh
a-*vayr*-es).

Poverty is no disgrace, but also no great honor – *Orem
iz nit kayn shand, ober oych kayn groisser koved nit* (O-
Rem iz nit *kayn shand*, o-*ber* oych *kayn* grois-er *kov*-ed
nit).

Hard to hold on to your money

My money went down the drain – *In drerd meyn geytl* (In
drerd meyn *geyt*-el).

It's easier to earn money than to keep it – *Gelt tsu fardinen
iz gringer vi tsu haltn* (Gelt tsu far-*din*-en iz *gring*-er vi tsu
halt-en).

Money is round; it rolls away from you – *Gelt is keylechdik;
amol iz es do, amol iz es dort* (Gelt is key-*lich*-dik; a-*mol* iz
es do, a-*mol* iz es dort).

Don't boast of money because you can easily lose it – *Mit
gelt tor men nit stolzyern, veyl me ken es gleych farleyren*
(Mit gelt or men nit *stolz*-yer-en, veyl me ken es *gleych* far-
leyr-en).

God should help you to see everything and not have the wherewithal to buy anything – *Got zol dir hedfen dee zolstu altsdeng, zen un nit hobn far vos tsu koyfn* (*Got* zol dir *hed*-fen dee *zols*-tu *alts*-deng, zen un nit *hob*-en far vos tsu *koyf*-en).

12
The Ultimate Yiddish Curse— Drop Dead!

Wishing someone would just drop dead is the ultimate Yiddish curse, and there are lots of ways of saying it. You can do it simply by saying "Bury yourself!" — *Lig in drerd!* (Lig in *drerd!*) or "Ver derharget!" (Get killed!) (Ver der-*har*-get!)

You can also do it more creatively with phrases like:

May someone call a doctor for you urgently, and when he arrives, they should inform him that it is too late – *Me zol rufn tsu dir srotshne a dokter un az iener vet kumen zol men im zogn az me darf shoyn nit* (Mit zol *ruf*-en tsu dir *srotsh*-ne a *dok*-ter un az i-*en*-er vet).

or

May there be a great fair in Paradise and may you be very successful there – *Zol shoyn zany a groyser irid in gen-eden, un zolst dortn matslich shem* (Zol *shoyn* za-ny a *groys*-er i-*rid* in gen-e-*den* un zolst *dort*-en *mats*-lich shem).

or

God should bless you with three persons: one should hold you, the second should kill you and the third should bury you – *Got zol dir bentshn mit dray mentshn: eyner zol dir haltn, der tsveyter zol dir shpaltn un der driter zol dir id bahaltn* (*Got* zol dir *bent*-shen mit dray *ment*-shin: ey-ner zol dir *halt*-en, der *tsveyt*-er zol dir *shpalt*-en un der *drit*-er zold dir ba-*halt*-en).

You'll find a great variety of options to tell someone to drop dead, go to hell, go to the devil, meet the Angel of Death, and you will find creative ways to suggest that someone be buried or look forward to mourning someone. Here are a bunch of Yiddish phrases for wishing someone an early death:

Telling someone to drop dead . . .

Drop dead – *Zolst lign in drerd* (Zolst *lig*-en in *drerd*).

Do me a favor and drop dead – *Folg mich a gang un gai in drerd* (*Folg* mich a *gong* un *gay* in *drerd*).

Drop dead – *Ver derharget* (*Ver* der-*har*-get).
Also can mean: Bury yourself! Go kill yourself!

Drop dead – *Geharget zolstu verren* (Geh-*har*-get *zolst*-u *ver*-en).
Literally means: You should get killed.

Drop dead – *Ich hob dich* (Ich hob dich).

He should drop dead – *Paygeren zol er* (Pay-*ger*-en zol er).

Drop dead – *Zol dir got arayngebn a naye neshumah un tsuhemen di alte* (Zol dir got a-*rhine*-geb-en a *naye* ne-*shum*-ah un tsu-*hem*-en di *al*-the).

Literally means: May God give you a new soul and take your old one.

May you be a dead duck tonight – *A kaporeh zolstu veren hayntike nacht* (A ka-*por*-eh *zols*-tu *ver*-en *hayn*-ti-ke).

May you push up daisies soon – *Groz zol oyf dir vaksn* (Groz zol oyf dir *vaks*-en).

May you be spared the indignities and illnesses of old age – *Zolst farshporn di bizoynut un di krenh fun der elter* (*Zolst* far-*shpor*-en di bi-*zoyn*-ut un *kren*-eh fun der *elt*-er).

If you want to avoid old age, hang yourself in youth – *Az me vil nit alt verren, zol men zich yungerhayt oyfhengn* (Az me vil nit alt *ver*-en zol, men zich yun-*ger*-hayt oyf-*heng*-en).

Hang yourself with a sugar rope and you'll have a sweet death – *Heng dich oyf a tsikershtrikl vestu hobn a zisn toyt* (*Heng* dich oyf a tsi-*ker*-shtrikl *ves*-tu *hob*-en a *zis*-en *toyt*).

May you suffer a cruel and unusual death – *A miteh-meshuneh zolstu hobn* (A *mit*-eh-me-*shun*-eh *zols*-tu *hob*-en).

Telling someone to go to hell . . .

Go to hell – *Gai in drerd arayn* (*Gay* in *drerd* a-*rhine*).

Go to hell – *Gai kabenyeh matyreh* (Gay ka-*ben*-yeh ma-*tyr*-eh).

Go to hell – *Ich hob dich in drerd* (*Ich* hob dich in *drerd*).

Go to hell – *In drerd mitten kop* (In *drerd mit*-en *kop*).
Literally means: Be in the ground up to your head.

Go to hell – *Gey tsu al dee gute-ior* (Gey tsu al dee *gut*-e-ior).
Literally means: Go to all the demons.

Go to hell [and bake bagels there] – *Lign drerd [un bak beygel]* (*Lig*-en *dred* [un bak *beyg*-el]).
Literally means: Live underground and bake bagels there.

Go to hell together with your bones – *Gey in drerd mit dee beyner* (*Gey* in *drerd* mit dee *beyn*-er).

He should go to hell – *Er zol einemen a miesseh meshuneh* (Er zol ein-*em*-en a *mies*-eh me-*shun*-eh).
Literally means: He should meet a strange death.

He should go to hell – *Er zol gayn in drerd* (Er zol *gayn* in *drerd*).

He should go to hell – *A gehenem oyf ihm* (A ge-*hen*-em oyf ihm).

Telling someone to go to the devil . . .

Go to the devil – *A ruech in dein tatn's tatenarein* (A *ru*-ech in dein *tat*-en's *tat*-en-a-rhine).

Go to the devil – *A ruech in dein tatn's tateh* (A *ru*-ech in dein *tat*-en's *ta*-teh).

May the Devil carry you on his shoulders – *Trogn zol did*

der ruech oyf di pleytses (*Trog*-en zol did der *ru*-ech oyf di
pleyts-es).

May the Devil [the cotton-wool maker] take you – *Chapt
did der ruech* [*dir vate-macher*] (*Chapt* did der *ru*-ech [dir
va-te-*ma*-cher]).
    The cotton-wool maker is a popular Yiddish euphemism
for the Devil.

Wishing someone meets the Angel of Death

May the Angel of Death fall in love with you – *Der malechamo'ves zol zid id dir farlibn* (Der me-*lech*-a-mo'ves zol
zid dir far-*lib*-en).

May the Angel of Death remove you from this world – *Der
malechamo'ves zol did tsunemen fun der velt* (Der ma-*lech*-
a-mo'ves zol did tsu-*nem*-en fun der *velt*).

May you romp with the Angel of Death – *Mitn malechamo'ves zolstu zid shpeln* (*Mit*-en ma-*lech*-a-mo'ves *zols*-
tu zid *shpel*-en).

He should marry the daughter of the Angel of Death –
Khasene hobn zol er mit di malech hamoves tochter (*Khas*-
en-eh *hob*-en zol er mit di *ma*-lech ha-*mov*-es *toch*-ter).

Finding creative burial methods

Go bury yourself – *Leyg zin in drerd arayn* (*Leyg* zin in
drerd a-*rhine*).

Go to the black pit – *Gey tsum shvare-ior* (*Gey* tsum *shvar*-
eh-i-or).

I will bury you in the ground as though you were a trea-
sure – *Id vel did bagrobn in der erd vi an oyster* (Id vel did
ba-*grog*-en in der erd vi an *oyst*-er).

May you be buried nine feet deep in the ground – *Ver
bagrobn nayn eyln in der erd* (Ver ba-*grog*-en *nayn eyl*-en in
der erd).

May you be carried out on a dead man's stretcher – *Trogn
zol men did oyf der miteh* (*Trog*-en zol men did oyf der
mit-eh).

I should outlive him long enough to bury him – *Vi tsu
derleb ich im shoyn tsu bagrobn* (Vi tsu *der*-leb ich im *shoy*-
en tsu ba-*grob*-en).

May you not stand in a cemetery, only lie there – *Oyf keyn
guten-ort zolstu nit shteyn nor lign* (Oyf *keyn gut*-en-ort *zols*-
tu nit *shtey*-en nor *lig*-en).

Looking forward to mourning someone

I hope to see you dead – *Id zol hobn a zchut bay got, er
zol did tsunenen fun der erd* (Id zol *hob*-en a *zchut* bay got,
er zol did tsu-*nem*-en fun der erd).
    Literally means: May God grant me the favor of removing
you from this world.

I wish you a sweet death: a truck full of sugar should run
over you – *A zisn toyt zolstu hobn a trok mit tsuker zoldid
iberforn* (A *zis*-en *toyt zols*-tu *hob*-en a trok mit *tsuk*-er *zol*-
did i-*ber*-forn).

Black sorrow is all that his mother should see of him –

Finstere leyd zol nor di mama oyf im zen. (Fin-*ster*-eh leyd zol nor di *ma*-ma oyf im zen).

May I have the privilege of sewing your shroud – *A soyve zol id dir machn* (A *soyv*-eh zol id dir *mach*-en).

May I grieve after you – *A brod zol in nod dir hobn* (A *brod* zol in *nod* dir).

May I mourn your death – *Id zol veyn oyf dayne iorn* (Id zol *veyn* oyf *dayne* i-orn).

May prayers be offered up for your soul – *Me zol did trogn un zingn* (Me zol did *trog*-en un *zing*-en).
   Literally means: May you be carried away amidst song.

May it end badly for you – *Zol es dir aroys bokem* (Zol es dir a-*roys bok*-em).

Why bother getting up alive – *Farshporn zol er oyf tsu shteyn* (*Farsh*-porn zol er oyf tsu *shteyn*)?

A young child should be named after him – *A kleyn kind zol noch im heysn* (A *kleyn* kind zol *noch* im *heys*-en).

English
to Yiddish
Glossary

English	Yiddish	How You Say It
A black year!	*A shvartz yor!*	A *Shvartz* yor!
A boil is fine as long as it's under someone else's arm.	*A geshvir iz a gutch zach bei yenem unhern orem.*	A *gesh*-vir iz a *gutch* zach bei *yen*-em un-hern o-*rem*.
A cramp in his body [in his stomach; in his guts; in his bowels; in his fingers and toes)].	*A kramp im in layb [in boyach; in di kishkes; in di gederem; in di finger].*	A *kramp* in *layb* [in *boy*-ach, in di *keesh*-kes, in di *ged*-er-em, in di *fing*-er].
A cramp in your stomach.	*A kramp dir in boyd.*	A *kramp* dir in *boyd*.
A fever should toss you (in bed) a foot high each time.	*Varfn zol did eylenvayz.*	Var-*fen* zol did ey-*len*-wayz.
A fire should strike you while you are speaking now.	*A fyer zol did trefn vee du redst.*	A *fy*-er did *tref*-en vee du *redst*.
A friend you can get for nothing; an enemy has to be bought.	*A freint bekamt men umzist; a soineh muz men zich koifn.*	A *freint bek*-amt men um-*zist*; a *soi*-neh muz men zich *koif*-en.
A friend you have to buy; enemies you get for nothing.	*A freint darf men zich koifn; sonem kright men umzist.*	A *freint* darf men zich *koif*-en; *son*-em *kright* men um-*zist*.

English	Yiddish	How You Say It

A horrible end should befall you — *A finsteren sof.* — A *fin*-ster-en *sof.*
Also can mean: May there be a dark ending for you.

A hundred houses shall he have; in every house a hundred rooms and in every room twenty beds, and a delirious fever should drive him from bed to bed.
Hindert hayzer zol er hobn; in yeder hoyz a hindert tsimern, in yeder tsimer tsvonsik betn un kadukhes zol im varfn fin eyn bet in der tsveyter.
Hind-ert hay-zer zol er *hob*-en; in *yed*-er *hoyz* a *hind*-ert *tsim*-ern in *yed*-er *tsim*-er *tsvon*-sik *bet*-en un ka-*duch*-es zol im *varf*-en fin eyn bet in der *tsveyt*-er.

A plague on you. — *A choleryeh oyf dir.* — A cho-*ley*-er-yeh oyf dir.

A plague on you. — *A finsteren yor.* — A *fin*-ster-en *yor.*
Literally means: A dark year (for you).

A plague should befall you. — *A magaifeh zol dich trefen.* — A ma-*gay*-feh *zol* dich *tref*-en.

A rope around your neck. — *A shtrek dir oyfn haldz.* — A *shtrek* dir oyf-en *haldz.*

A stabbing pain in your stomach. — *A shnaydenish dir in boyd.* — A *shnay*-de-nish dir in *boyd.*

A wise man knows what he says, a fool says what he knows. — *A kluger vaist vos er zogt, a nar zogt vos er vaist.* — A *klug*-er *vaist* vos er zogt, a *nar* zogt vos er *vaist.*

A young child should be named after him. — *A kleyn kind zol noch im heysn.* — A *kleyn* kind zol *noch* im *heys*-en.

All his teeth should fall out except one to make him suffer. — *Ale tseyn zoln bay im aroysfalen, not eyner zol im blayben oyf tsonveytung.* — Ale *tseyn zoln* bay im a-*roys*-fal-en not *eyn*-er zol in *blayb*-en oyf tson-*veyt*-ung.

English	Yiddish	How You Say It
All problems I have in my heart should go to his head.	*Ale tsores vos ich hob oyf mayn hartsn zoln oysgeyn tsu zayn kop.*	Ale *tsor-*es vos ich hob oyf *may-*en *harts-*en, zoln *oysg-*eyn tsu *zhine* kop.
All the troubles (that weigh down my heart) should fall on your head.	*Ale tsores (vos id hob oyf mayn hartn) zoln oysgeyn tsu dayn kop.*	Ale *tsor-*es (vos id *hob* oyf *mayn hart-*en) zoln osy-*gey-*en tsu *dayn kop.*

An ugly ending to you.　*Miesseh meshuneh.*　*Meese-*eh ma-*shee-*neh.
　　Also means: To wish lots of trouble on someone. Literally means: A
　　strange death or a tragic end.

Annoying person　　*Nudnik*　　*Nood-*nik
　　Also can be used to refer to someone who is a bore, is being
　　obnoxious, nagging you, or generally being a nuisance.

Are you crazy?　　*Tsi bistu meshugeh?*　Tsi-*bis-*tu me-*shug-*eh?

| As many years as he's walked on his feet, let him walk on his hands, and for the rest of the time he should crawl along on his ass. | *Vifil yor er iz gegangn oyf di fis zol er geyn af di hent un di iberike zol er zich sharn oyf di hintn.* | Vi-fil yor er iz ge-*gang-*en oyf di fis zol er *geyn* af hi *hent* un di i-*ber-*ike zol er zich *sharn* oyf di *hint-*en. |

As you make your bed,　*Vi me bet zich oys,*　Vi me bet *zich* oys, a-
so will you sleep in it.　*azoy darf men shlofn.*　*zoy* darf men *shlof-*en.

Ass kisser　　*Toches-lecker*　　*Too-*ches *leck-*er
　　Also can refer to a brown-noser or someone who will do anything to
　　gain favor. Literally means: buttock-licker.

Bagel　　*Beygl*　　*Bay-*gul
　　Probably one of the most popular Jewish foods that has found its
　　way into many American hearts. It's a hard, ring-shaped bread roll
　　that finds its roots in the Middle High German word *bougel.*

English	Yiddish	How You Say It

Bastard   *Mamzer*   *Mamz*-er
  Also someone who is a nasty, unworthy person.

Better a crooked foot   *Beser a krumer fus*   *Bes*-er a *krum*-er fus
than a crooked mind.   *ayder a krumer kop.*   ay-*der* a *krum*-er *kop.*

Better that you should *Zolst beser lebn—un* *Zolst bes*-er *leb*-en—un
live and suffer.   *mutshen zid.*   mut-*shen* zid.

Better to do nothing   *Beser dos kind zol*   *Bes*-er dos kind *zol*
than to make   *vaynen ayder der*   *vayn*-en ay-*der* der
something into   *foter.*   *fot*-er
nothing.

Bialy   *Bialy*   Bee-*ya*-lee
  Roll, shaped like a disc, which is thicker around the outer edges and
  flattened in the middle. The middle of a *bialy* is traditionally filled
  with onion pieces and sometimes cheese. It gets its name from the
  Polish city Bialystok, which is credited with its creation.

Big deal, so what.   *Groisser gehilleh.*   *Groys*-eh geh-*hill*-eh.

Big idiot   *Groisser putz*   *Groys*-er putz
  Also: big prick, big penis, big fool or big shot.

Big good-for-nothing.   *Groisser gornisht.*   *Groys*-er *gor*-nisht.

Bimbo   *Tzatzkeh*   *Tzatz*-keh
  Also can refer to someone who is a mistress, sexually attractive girl,
  or an overdressed woman. Another meaning can be a toy, ornament
  or expensive plaything.

Black sorrow is all that *Finstere leyd zol nor di* Fin-*ster*-eh leyd zol nor
his mother should see   *mama oyf im zen.*   di *ma*-ma oyf im zen.
of him.

Blintz   *Blintse*   Blint-seh
  Looks like a thick crepe or thin pancake that's folded around some
  type of filling. Cheese, potatoes and fruit, individually or combined,

English	Yiddish	How You Say It

are the most common fillings used. Its origin is in the Russian word *blinets* or "little pancake."

| Braggart | *Shvitzer* | *Shvitz*-er |

Literally means: Someone who sweats.

| Burst | *Plotz* | *Plots* |

When you feel like you are ready to explode from too much excitement or anger, you can say, "I want to plotz."

| Butter-fingered | *Shlemiel* | Shleh-*meal* |

Also an inept or foolish person, a simpleton, nincompoop or a bungler.

| Choke on it. | *Ver dershtikt.* | *Vair* der-*shtikt.* |

| Clumsy person | *Shmuck* | *Shmuck* |

Shmuck means a clumsy or stupid person. This comes from the Yiddish word *shmock*, which means penis or fool, but some think its beginnings are actually in the Polish word *smok*, which means serpent or tail.

| Clumsy person | *Klutz* | *Klutz* |

Also a stupid person or a dolt

| Comedy act | *Shtik* | *Shtik* |

Piece or routine. An entertainment routine, usually a comedy act. Its origins are from High Middle German word, *stucke* or piece.

| Complainer | *Kvetcher* | *Kvetch*-er |

Also can refer to someone who is a whiner. Nothing is ever good enough for them. Rodney Dangerfield was known as the king of the *kvetchers*. *Kvetch* in Yiddish means to squeeze.

| Confused person | *Farblondjet* | Far-*blond*-jet |

When you think someone is totally confused, you can say they are *farblondjet*. Also used when you think someone is lost.

English	Yiddish	How You Say It
Crazy bastard	*Meshugener mamzer*	Meh-*shu*-gen-er *mamzer*

Its roots are from the Hebrew word *meshugga* (meh-*shu*-ga) for crazy and *mamzer* for bastard.

Dirt	*Shmutz*	*Shmutz*

Lots of dirt or slime.

Do me a favor and drop dead.	*Folg mich a gang un gai in drerd.*	*Folg* mich a *gong* un *gay* in *drerd.*

Don't aggravate me.	*Tsap mir nit dos blut.*	*Tsap* meer nit *dos blut.*

Literally means: Don't bleed me.

Don't be a fool.	*Zeit nit kain goylem.*	*Zye* nit kane *go*-lem.

Also can mean: Don't be a robot.

Don't be a fool.	*Zeit nit kain nar.*	*Zye* nit kane *nar.*

Don't be an idiot.	*Zei nit kain vyzoso.*	*Zye* nit kane vi-*zo*-so.

Also can mean: Don't be a damn fool, or Don't be a penis.

Don't boast of money because you can easily lose it.	*Mit gelt tor men nit stolzyern, veyl me ken es gleych farleyren.*	Mit gelt or men nit *stolz*-yer-en, veyl me ken es *gleych* far-*leyr*-en.

Don't bother me.	*Hak mir nit kain cheinik.*	*Hak* meer nit *kayn chy*-nik.

Literally means: Don't bang on the teakettle.

Don't bother me.	*Drai mir nit kain kop.*	*Dray* meer nit *kayn kop.*

Literally means: Don't twist my head.

Don't bother me.	*Chepeh zich nit tsu mir.*	*Chep*-eh zich nit *tsu* meer.

Literally means: Don't attach yourself to me!

English	Yiddish	How You Say It
Don't bother me.	*Chepeh zich op fun mir.*	*Chep*-eh zich *op* fun meer.
Don't butt in. Keep your nose out of it.	*Mish zich nisht arayn.*	*Mish* zich *nisht* a-*rhine*.

Don't fuck with me.   *Bareh nit.*   *Bar*-eh nit.
Also means: Don't fornicate around, but more mildly can mean, Don't fool around, don't annoy or don't bother someone.

| Don't threaten me | *Strasheh mich nit.* | *Stra*-sheh mich nit. |

Dreamer   *Luftmensh*   *Luft*-mensh
Also can refer to someone who is an unrealistic optimist; builds castles in the air and has no trade or income. You definitely don't want to loan money to a person like this for their next big scheme to make money. Literally means: Air man.

| Drive yourself crazy. | *Gai fardray zich dein aigenem kop.* | *Gay far*-dray *zich dine* eye-*gen-em kop* |
| Drop dead. | *Zolst lign in drerd.* | Zolst *lig*-en in *drerd.* |

Drop dead.   *Geharget zolstu verren.*   Geh-*har*-get *zolst*-u ver-en.
Literally means: You should get killed.

Drop dead.   *Zol dir got arayngebn a naye neshumah un tsuhemen di alte.*   Zol dir got a-*rhine*-geb-en a *naye* ne-*shum*-ah un tsu-*hem*-en di *al*-the.
Literally means: May God give you a new soul and take your old one.

| Drop dead. | *Ich hob dich.* | Ich hob dich. |

Drop dead.   *Ver derharget.*   *Ver* der-*har*-get.
Also can mean: Bury yourself. Go kill yourself.

English	Yiddish	How You Say It

Drunkard   *Shikker*   *Shik*-er
Someone who is a drunkard, is a *shikker*. Its origins are in the
Hebrew word *sikkor* or *sakar*, "to be drunk."

Dull-witted   *Poyer*   *Poy*-er
Also can refer to a peasant, farmer, boor or dullard.

Dumbbell or dunce *Dumkop*   *Dum*-kop
Literally means: Dumb head.

Expert   *Maven*   *May*-vin
When you think someone is an expert, you can call him a *maven*.
Also used to indicate someone is an authority on a subject or a
connoisseur.

Finished fucking?   *Shoyn opgetrent?*   *Shoin op*-geh-trent?
Also translates to: Are you finished screwing around? Or, Have you
finished the dirty work? Literally means: Have you finished fornicating?

Fooey   *Feh*   *Fay*
Multipurpose word that can mean "Fooey!"; "That's terrible!"; "I hate
that!"; "That stinks!"; or "How disgusting!"

Fool or idiot   *Putz*   *Putz*

For the smallest favor   *Far der klenster toyveh*   Far der *klenst*-er *toyv-*
you become a debtor.   *vert men a ba'al-choyv.*   eh vert men a ba'al-
                                                         choyv.

Fortune makes you   *Der mazel macht klug,*   Der *maz*-el macht *klug,*
smart, because fortune   *veil der mazel macht*   veil der *maz*-el macht
makes you rich.   *reich.*   *reich.*

From fortune to mis-   *Fun glik tsum umglik*   Fun *glik* tsum um-*glik*
fortune is a short   *iz a shpan; fun umglik*   iz a *shpan*; fun um-
step; from misfortune   *tsum glik iz a shtik*   *glik* iz a *shtik* veg.
to fortune is a long   *veg.*
way.

English	Yiddish	How You Say It
From litigation you can never recover your loss.	*Az me tut zich lodn, kumt men sey vi nit tsum shodn.*	Az me tut zich *lod*-en, kumt men sey vi nit tsum *shod*-en.
From overeating one suffers more than from not eating enough.	*Fun iberessn cholyet men mer vi fun nit deressn.*	Fun i-*ber*-es-sen *chol*-yet men mer vi fun nit *der*-es-sen.

Full of shit	*Farcockt*	Far-*cocked*

Shitty or badly soiled. When you think someone is full of shit, you can say, "You're *farcockt*."

Gefilte fish	*Gefilte*	Ge-*fil*-te

Stuffed fish. It's made by using a whole fish, then chopping the fish meat into very small pieces. Most often, carp, pike or salmon is used and sometimes a mixture of more than one of these types of fish. Other common ingredients include onions, celery, carrots, sugar, white pepper, salt, eggs and matzo meal. The mixture is then stuffed back into the fish's skin or body cavity (bones and all) and boiled or baked. Today most people just buy balls of gefilte fish mixture in jars or cans, and you will find it on the dinner table at all Jewish holiday celebrations.

Get lost.	*Ver farblondjet.*	*Vair* far-*blond*-jet.

Give a pig a chair, he'll want to get on the table.	*Az me lozt a chazzer aruf af'n bank, viler af'n tish.*	Az me *lozt* a *chazz*-er a-ruf af'n *bank* vil-er af'n *tish.*

Gloat	*Kvell*	K-vell

Used when you are gloating over your children to show pride in their accomplishments. Someone might also *kvell* when they are enjoying an enemy's bad luck.

Go bang your head against the wall.	*Gai klop zich kop in vant.*	*Gay klop* zich *kop* in *vant.*

English	Yiddish	How You Say It
Go bother the bedbugs.	*Gai bareh di vantsen.*	*Gay bar*-eh di *vant*-sen.
Go break a leg.	*Gai tsebrech a fus.*	*Gay* tse-*brech* a foos.
Go break you own head.	*Shlog zich kog in vant.*	*Shlog* zich *kog* in *vant.*
Go bury yourself.	*Leyg zin in drerd arayn.*	*Leyg* zin in *drerd* a-*rhine.*
Go drive yourself crazy.	*Fardray zich dayn aygenem kop.*	Far-*dray* zich *dayn* ay-*gen*-em kop.
Go drive yourself crazy.	*Gai fardrai zich deyn kop.*	*Gay* far-*dray* zich *deyn kop.*
Go drown.	*Ich hob dich in bod.*	Ich *hob* dich in *bod.*

Literally: I have you in the bath.

English	Yiddish	How You Say It
Go fuck yourself.	*Gai tren zich.*	*Gay tren* zich.
Go jump in a lake.	*Nem zich a vaneh.*	Nem zich a *van*-eh.

Literally means: Go take a bath.

English	Yiddish	How You Say It
Go mix yourself up, not me.	*Gai fardray zich dayn aigenem kop.*	*Gay* far-*dray* zich *dayn* ay-*gen*-em kop.
Go screw up your head.	*Fardrai zich dem kop.*	Far-*dray* zich dem *kop.*
Go shit on the ocean.	*Gai cocken ahfen yam.*	*Gay cock*-en *ah*-fin yam.

Also can be used to mean: Don't bother me, or Get lost.

English	Yiddish	How You Say It
Go take a shit.	*Cock zich oys.*	*Cock* zich oys.

Also means: Go take a shit for yourself.

English	Yiddish	How You Say It
Go to hell and bake bagels there.	*Lign drerd un bak beygel.*	*Lig*-en *drerd* un bak *beyg*-el.

Literally means: Live underground and bake bagels there.

English	Yiddish	How You Say It
Go to hell together with your bones.	*Gey in drerd mit dee beyner.*	*Gey* in *drerd* mit dee *beyn*-er.
Go to hell.	*Gai kab enyeh mattereh.*	*Gay kab en*-yeh ma-*ter*-eh.
Go to hell.	*Gai in drerd arayn.*	*Gay* in *draird* a-*rhine*.

Literally means: Go down into the earthly grave.

English	Yiddish	How You Say It
Go to hell!	*Ich hob dich in drerd!*	Ich *hob* dich in *draird*.
Go to hell.	*Gai kabenyeh matyreh.*	*Gay* ka-*ben*-yeh ma-*tyr*-eh.
Go to hell.	*In drerd mitten kop.*	In *drerd mit*-en *kop*.

Literally means: Be in the ground up to your head.

English	Yiddish	How You Say It
Go to hell.	*Gey tsu al dee gute-ior.*	Gey tsu al dee *gut*-e-ior.

Literally means: Go to all the demons.

English	Yiddish	How You Say It
Go to the black pit.	*Gey tsum shvare-ior.*	*Gey* tsum *shvar*-eh-i-or.
Go to the devil.	*A ruech in dein tatn's tatenarein.*	A *ru*-ech in dein *tat*-en's *tat*-en-a-rhine.
Go to the devil.	*A ruech in dein tatn's tateh.*	A *ru*-ech in dein *tat*-en's *ta*-teh.
God helps the poor man; he protects him from expensive sins.	*Got helft dem oreman: er farhit im fun tey'ereh avayres.*	*Got* helft dem o-*re*-man: er *far*-hit im fun tey'er-eh a-*vayr*-es.

English	Yiddish	How You Say It
God should bestow him with everything his heart desires, but he should be a quadriplegic and not be able to use his tongue.	*Got zol gebn, er zol hobn altsding vos zayn harts glist, nor er zol zayn geleymt oyf ale ayvers un nit kenen rirn mit der tsun.*	*Got* zol *geb*-en er zol *hob*-en *alts*-ding vos zhine *harts glist*, nor er zol *zayn* ge-*leymt* oyf ale ay-vers un nit *ken*-en rirn mit der *tsun*.
God should bless you with three persons: one should hold you, the second should kill you and the third should bury you.	*Got zol dir bentshn mit dray mentshn: eyner zol did haltn, der tsveyter zol did shpaltn un der driter zold id bahaltn.*	*Got* zol dir *bent*-shen mit dray *ment*-shin: ey-ner zol did *halt*-en, der *tsveyt*-er zol di *shpalt*-en un der *drit*-er zold id ba-*halt*-en.
God should help you to see everything and not have the wherewithal to buy anything.	*Got zol dir helfen dee zolstu altsdeng, zen un nit hobn far vos tsu koyfn.*	*Got* zol dir *hel*-fen dee zols-tu *alts*-deng, zen un nit *hob*-en far vos tsu *koyf*-en.
God should visit upon him the best of the Ten Plagues.	*Got zol oyf im onshikn fin di tsen makes di beste.*	*Got zol oyf in* onsh-*ikn fin di tsen* mak-*es di* bes-*te*.

Good deed   *Mitzvah*   *Mits*-veh

A good deed. When you do something to help someone else, it's called a *mitzvah*.

Good health.   *Gezunt-heit.*   Ge-*zunt*-heit.

Commonly used when someone sneezes, sometimes in conjunction with "God bless you." You can also use it as part of a toast.

Good luck.   *Mazel tov.*   *Ma*-zel tov.

Mazel means luck and *Tov* means good. Also used to say Congratulations!

English	Yiddish	How You Say It

Gossip   *Yenta*   *Yen*-teh
Also can refer to someone who is a busybody, talkative woman or
blabbermouth.

Greasy   *Shmaltz*   *Shmaltz*
Melted fat. Usually used to refer to something that is greasy, gooey
or has lots of fat drippings. But, you'll also hear it when someone is
talking about something corny or overly sentimental. In that case a
"y" is added at the end. For example, "Wasn't that a *shmaltzy* play?"
Some people also use *shmaltzy* to describe something as flattery,
sweet talk or overpraise. For example, "Wasn't that a *shmaltzy*
introduction?" Its origins are in the German word *schmaltz* of the
same meaning.

Halvah   *Halvah*   Hal-*vah*
Sweetmeat. Claimed not only by the Jews, but many Middle Eastern
cultures. It originated in the Balkans and eastern Mediterranean
regions. It's made with sesame seeds and honey or sugar syrup.
Other ingredients can be added, such as dried fruit, pistachio nuts
and almonds. Some people add cinnamon and cardamom. The
ingredients are blended together, heated and poured into bars or
loaves. In addition to the Yiddish word *halvah*, Turkish call it *helva*,
Greeks call it *halva*, Arabs call it *halwa* or *halawi*. In each case it
translates to "sweetmeat."

Hang yourself with a sugar rope and you'll have a sweet death.	*Heng dich oyf a tsikershtrikl vestu hobn a zisn toyt.*	*Heng* dich oyf a tsi-*ker*-shtrikl *ves*-tu *hob*-en a *zis*-en *toyt.*
He should be transformed into a chandelier, to hang by day and to burn by night.	*Migulgl zol er vern in a henglayhter, bay tog zol er hengn, un bay nacht zol er brenen.*	Mi-*gul*-gel zol er *vern* in a heng-*layht*-er, bay tog zol er *heng*-en, un bay *nacht* zol er *bren*-en.
He should break a leg.	*Zol er tzebrechne a fus.*	Zol er tze-*brech*-en a foos.

English	**Yiddish**	**How You Say It**
He should burn up.	*A fyer zol im trefn.*	A *fy-*er zol im *tref-*en.
He should crap blood and pus.	*Er zol kakn mit blit un mit ayter.*	Er zol *kak-*en mit *blit* un mit *ayt-*er.
He should drink too much castor oil.	*Azoy fil ritzinoyl zol er oystrinkn.*	A-*zoy* fil rit-*zin-*oyl zol er oy-*strink-*en.
He should drop dead.	*Paygeren zol er.*	Pay-*ger-*en zol er.
He should get so sick as to cough up his mother's milk.	*Oyskrinkn zol er dus mame's milach.*	Oy-*strink-*en zol er dus *ma-*me's *mil-*ach.
He should give it all away to doctors.	*Oyf doktoyrim zol er dos avekgebn.*	Oyf *dok-*toy-rim zol er dos a-*vek-*geb-en.
He should go to hell.	*A gehenem oyf im.*	A geh-*hen-*em oyf *im.*
He should go to hell.	*Er zol gayn in drerd.*	Er zol *gayn* in drerd.
He should grow a wooden tongue.	*A hiltsener tsung zol er bakumn.*	A hil-*tsen-*er zol er ba-*kumn.*
He should grow like an onion with his head in the ground.	*Er zol vakesen vi a tsibeleh, mit dem kop in drerd.*	Er zol *vakes* en vi a *tsib-*el-eh, mit dem *kop* in drerd.
He should have a large store, and whatever people ask for he shouldn't have, and what he does have shouldn't be requested.	*A groys gesheft zol er hobn mit shroyre: vus er hot, zol men bay im nit fregn, un vos men fregt zol er nisht hobn.*	A *groys* ge-*sheft* zol er *hob-*en mit *shroy-*re: vus er hot, zol men bay im nit *freg-*en, un vos men *fregt* zol er nisht hob-en.
He should have lots of trouble.	*Er zol zain ayf tsores.*	Er zol *zain* ayf *tsor-*es.

English	Yiddish	How You Say It
He should have lots of trouble.	*Er zol ainemen a miesseh meshuneh.*	Er zol ai-*ne*-men a *mies*-eh *mesh*-un-eh.
He should have lots of trouble.	*Aleh tsores oyf zein kop.*	Al-eh *tsor*-es oyf zine kop.
He should marry the daughter of the Angel of Death.	*Khasene hobn zol er mit di malech hamoves tochter.*	*Khas*-en-eh *hob*-en zol er mit di *ma*-lech ha-*mov*-es *tocht*-er.
He should see everything, but have no reason (with which) to buy it.	*Er zol altsting zen, un nit hobn farvos (mit vos) tsu koyfn.*	*Er zol* als-*ting zen, un nit* hob-*en far-vos (mit vos) tsu* koyf-*en.*
He talks himself into sickness.	*Er redt zich eyn a krenk.*	Er *redt* zich eyn a krenk.
He who keeps quiet is half a fool; he who talks is a complete fool.	*Az me shvaygt iz men a halber nar; az me redt iz men a gantser nar.*	Az me *shvagt* iz men a *halb*-er nar; az me *redt* iz men a *gants*-er nar.
He who lives with the devil, becomes a devil.	*Az me lebt mit a tayvel, vert men a tayvel.*	Az me *lebt* mit a *tayv*-el, vert men a tayv-el.
He who throws stones on another gets them back on his own bones.	*Ver es varft oil yenem shteyner krigt tsurik in di aigneh bainer.*	Ver es varft oil yen-em shteyn-er krigt tsur-ik in di aig-neh bain-er.
Hello	*Shalom*	*Sha*-lom

Hebrew word with lots of different meanings including, hello, peace, good-bye, so long and other similar words of welcome when someone comes in, or good-bye when someone leaves. But it's only good-bye until you can welcome someone again.

English	Yiddish	How You Say It
His luck should be as bright as a new moon.	*Zayn mazel zol im layhtn vee dee levone in sof choydesh.*	*Zayn maz*-el zol im *layht*-en vee dee *lev*-one in sof *choy*-desh.

English	Yiddish	How You Say It

Hole in the head   *Loch in kop*   *Loch* in *kop*

Holy shit.   *Oy gevalt.*   *Oy* ge-*valt.*
Use it when you hear shocking news. It's usually used to express
alarm, dismay, fear, terror or astonishment. When used with "*oy*," it
can mean "That's dreadful!" or "Holy Shit!" The Yiddish origin is the
word *G'vald*, which means force or violence.

Honor   *Koved*   *Ko*-vid
When you hold high respect for someone or something, you are said
to *koved* it. *Koved* means respect, honor, revere or hold in high
esteem.

I despise you.   *Ich fief oyf dir!*   Ich *fife* oyf deer.
Literally means: I whistle on you.

I don't give a damn.   *Es hart mich vi di vant.*   Es *hart* mich vee dee
                                                                              vant.
Literally means: It bothers me like a wall.

I hope I can come to   *Id tsu dir oyf simchut,*   Id tsu dir oyf sim-*chut,*
you on joyous   *du tsu mir oyf kuliem.*   du tsu mir oy ku-*li*-em.
occasions and that
you will come to me
on crutches.

I hope to see you   *Id zol hobn a zchut bay*   Id zol hob-en a *zchut*
dead.   *got, er zol dir tsunenen*   bay got, er zol dir tsu-
          fun der erd.   *nem*-en fun der erd.
          Literally means: May God grant me the favor of removing you from
          this world.

I hope to see you on   *Id zol dir zen oyf eyn*   Id zol dir *zen* ofy eyn
one leg and may you   *fus un du mir mit eyn*   *fus* un du *mir* mit
see me with one eye.   *oyg.*   eyn *oyg.*

I need it like a hole in   *Ich darf es vi a loch in*   Ich *darf* es vee a *loch*
the head.   *kop.*   in *kop.*

English	Yiddish	How You Say It
I need it like a wart on my nose.	*Ich darf es vi a lung un leber oif der noz.*	Ich darf es vee a lung un *leb*-er oif der noz.
I shit on him.	*Ich cock ahf im.*	Ich cock ahf im.
I should outlive him long enough to bury him.	*Vi tsu derleb ich im shoyn tsu bagrobn.*	Vi tsu *der*-leb ich im *shoy*-en tsu ba-*grob*-en.
I will bury you in the ground as though you were a treasure.	*Id vel did bagrobn in der erd vi an oytser.*	Id vel did ba-*grog*-en in der erd vi an *oyts*-er.
I wish you a sweet death: a truck full of sugar should run over you.	*A zisn toyt zolstu hobn a trok mit tsuker zoldid iberforn.*	A *zis*-en *toyt zols*-tu *hob*-en a trok mit *tsuk*-er *zol*-did i-*ber*-forn.
I've got him by the ass.	*Ich hob im in toches.*	Ich *hob* im in *too*-ches.

Also can mean: I have him in my ass.

Idiot	*Shmegegi*	Shmeh-*geh*-gee

Also a nothing or a nobody

If anyone writes you, they should write you doctors' prescriptions.	*Shraybn zol men dir retseptn.*	*Shrayb*-en zol men dir re-tsept-en.
If one steals a lot of eggs, one can also become rich.	*Az men ganvet a sach ayer, ken men oich verren a nogid.*	Az men *gan*-vet a *sach* ay-er, *ken* men oich ver-ren a nog-id.
If you don't save the penny, you'll not have the dollar.	*Az me shport nit dem groshn, hot men nit dem rubel.*	Az me *shport* nit dem *grosh*-en, hot men nit dem *rub*-el.

English	Yiddish	How You Say It
If you have money, you are wise and good-looking and can sing well too.	*Az me hot gelt, iz men klug un shain un men ken gut zingn.*	*Az me hot gelt, iz men* klug *un* shain *un men* ken *gut* zing-*en.*
If you have the money, you have the say.	*Az men hot di matbayeh, hot men di dayeh.*	Az men hot di mat-*bay*-eh, hot men di day-eh.
If you invest in a fever, you will realize a disease.	*Az me laight arayn kadoches, nemt men aroyz a krenik.*	Az me *laight* a-*rhine* ka-*doch*-es, nemt men a-*royz* a kren-ik.
If you keep on talking, you will end up saying what you didn't intend to say.	*Az me redt, derredt men zich.*	Az me *redt, der*-redt men zich.
If you lie down with the dogs, you get up with the fleas.	*Az me shloft mit hint, shtayt men oyf mit flay.*	Az me *shloft* mit *hint* shtayt men *oyf* mit *flay.*
If you repeat often enough that you're right, you will discover you are wrong.	*Az men chazert tsu fil iber vi grecht men iz, vert men umgerecht.*	Az men *chaz*-ert tsu fil i-ber vi *grecht* men iz, vert men um-*ger*-echt.
If you tell a lie, may you lie ill.	*Oyb du zogst lign, zolstu krenk lign.*	Oyb du zogst *lig-en,* zols-tu *krenk* lig-en.
If you want to avoid old age, hang yourself in youth.	*Az me vil nit alt verren, zol men zich yungerhayt oyfhengen*	Az me vil nit alt ver-en zol, men zich yun-*ger*-hayt oyf-heng-en.
If you want to please everybody, you'll die before your time.	*Vest vellen zich oysfaynen far layt, vestu shtarbn far der tsayt.*	Vest vell-en zich oys-*fay*-nen far *layt, ves*-tu *shtrab*-en far der tsayt.

English	Yiddish	How You Say It
If you're a child at twenty, you're an ass at twenty-one.	*Az men iz biz tsvantsik yor a kind, iz men tsu ayn-un-tsvantsik a behaymeh.*	Az men iz biz *tsvant*-sik yor a *kind*, iz men tsu ayn un *tsvant*-sik a be-*hay*-meh.
If you're at odds with your rabbi, make peace with your bartender.	*Az men krigt zich mitn rov, muz men sholem zeyn mitn shainker.*	Az men *krigt* zich *mit*-en rov, muz men *shol*-en zyen *mit*-en *shaink*-er.

Impolite person   *Bulvan*   *Bul*-van
Also means: A rude or ill-mannered person.

Incompentent person   *Loy yitslach*   Loy yits-lach
Also can refer to someone who has perpetual bad luck.

Incompetent person   *Shlemazel*   Shleh-*mah*-zel
Also can refer to someone who has perpetual bad luck or misfortune.

Inexperienced person   *Pisher*   *Pish*-er
Also can be used to indicate someone is inexperienced, unseasoned or "wet behind the ears." Or for someone who thinks he's adult enough to handle a task, but really isn't. Another more literal meaning is bed-wetter.

Informer   *Mosser*   *Moo*-ser

Insane or crazy   *Mishegass*   Mih-sheh-*gas*
When everything is just crazy or gone insane, you can call it a big "*mishegass*." This is a variation of the Hebrew word *meshugga* (meh-*shu*-ga), which means crazy.

| It would have been better if a stone had come out of your mother's womb, rather than you. | *Beser volt oyf dyn ort a shteyn arayn.* | *Be*-ser volt oyf dyn *ort* a *shtey*-en a-rhine. |

English	Yiddish	How You Say It
It's easier to earn money than to keep it.	*Gelt tsu fardinen iz gringer vi tsu haltn.*	Gelt tsu far-*din*-en iz *gring*-er vi tsu halt-en.
It's useless. It'll help like bloodletting on a dead body.	*Es vet helfn vi a toitn bahnekes.*	Es vet *helf*-en vee a *toyt*-en *bahn*-kis.
Joy	*Naches*	*Nach*-es

Means joy or happiness. Used most often by parents who say their children give them great *naches*.

Kaiser roll	*Kaiser*	*Kai*-ser

Breakfast roll that is light and fluffy on the inside with a thin outer crust. It's made by using a square piece of dough and folding the corners of the dough into the center. Sometimes it's made with poppy seeds and sometimes without the seeds. The name for this roll actually comes from Germany, called *Kaisersemmel* for the German emperor, plus *semmel*, which means roll.

Kibbitz or Kibbitzer	*Kibbitz or Kibbitzer*	*Kib*-itz or *Kib*-itz-er

When someone talks too much or gets involved in a subject when they shouldn't, they're called a *kibbitzer*. *Kibbitz* usually means unsolicited or unwanted advice. A person that offers that advice is a *kibbitzer*, also known as a meddlesome spectator.

Kiss my ass.	*Kush mich in toches.*	*Kush* mich in *too*-ches.
Kiss my ass.	*Kush in toches arayn.*	*Kush* in *too*-ches a-rhine.
Knish	*Knish*	K-nish

Piece of dough stuffed with potato, meat or cheese and baked or fried, commonly eaten as a snack or an appetizer. Its origins are in the Ukrainian word *Knysh*.

English	Yiddish	How You Say It

Kosher   *Kosher*   *Ko*-sher
Conforming to dietary laws, when talking about food. Its origin is Hebrew and means fitting or proper. Today as slang it's used for nonfood items and means that the material is legitimate, permissible, genuine or authentic. For example, it's commonly used in phrases such as: "Using bikes on the path is *kosher,*" or "The story about New York is *kosher.*"

Kugel   *Kugel*   *Ku*-gel
Casserole-like dish made with noodles or potatoes then baked with eggs and seasoning. A sweet *kugel* can be made with noodles, raisins and apples. In Yiddish, *kugel* actually means ball, which related to its puffed-up or mound shape. The word originates in Middle High German.

Lazy man   *Foiler*   *Foy*-ler

Leave me alone.   *Loz mich tzu ru.*   *Loz* mich tzu *ru.*
Literally means: Let me be in peace.

Leave me alone.   *Chepeh zich op fun mir.*   *Chep*-eh zich *op* fun meer.
Also means: Get away from me.

Lecherous old man   *Alter kucker*   Al-ter *kuck*-er
Also means: Old fogy. Literally means: An old defecator.

Leeches should drink him dry.   *Trinkn zoln im piavkes.*   *Trink*-en zoln im piav-kes.

Let what I wish on him come true [most, even half, even just 10 percent].   *Zol es im onkumn vos ich vintsh im [chotsh a helft, chotsh halb, chotsh a tsent cheyli].*   Zol es im on-*kumn* vos ich *vintsh* im [*chotsh* a helft, chotsh halb, chotsh a *tsent chey*-li].

Liar   *Ligner*   *Lig*-ner

English	Yiddish	How You Say It
Life is the biggest bargain—we get it for nothing.	*Der lebn iz di gresteh metsi'eh—me wrigt es umzist.*	Der *leb*-en iz di *grest*-eh met-si'eh—me *wrigt* es um-zist.

Long-winded story   *Megillah*   Me-*gil*-lah
 When someone blows something way out of proportion, you can call
 it a big *megillah.* It's also used to express that someone has told you
 the entire story with complete details—many times in a very long-
 winded way. The word actually is the name of the story of Esther
 and read on the holiday of Purim.

| Lost years are worse than lost dollars. | *Farloreneh yoren iz erger vi a farloreneh gelt.* | Far-*lor*-en-eh *yor*-en iz *erg*-er vi a far-*lor*-en-eh gelt. |

Lox   *Laks*   *Laks*
 Smoked salmon, from the Yiddish word *laks*, which means salmon.
 This actually comes from the German word for salmon, *lachs*, which
 was taken from an Indo-European word meaning salmon.

| May a boil grow on your belly button. | *S'zol dir vaksn a geshver oyfn pupik.* | S'zol dir *vaks*-en a *gesh*-ver oyf-en poo-pik. |

| May a bone remain stuck in your throat. | *A beyn zol dir in haldz blayben shtekn.* | A *beyn* zol dir in *haldz* *blayb*-en *shtek*-en. |

| May a cannon ball split your skull. | *A harmat zol dayn kop tseshmetern.* | A *harm*-at zol *dayn kop* tsesh-*met*-ern. |

| May a demon take your father's father. | *A ruech in dayn tatns zun arayn* | A *ru*-ech in dayn *tat*-ens zun a-*rhine.* |

| May a disease enter his gums. | *A krenk zol im arayn in di yosles.* | A *krenk* zolim a-*rhine* in dee *yos*-lis. |

| May a fire burn in your guts. | *A brand dir in dee kishkes.* | A *brand* dir in dee *keesh*-kes. |

English	Yiddish	How You Say It
May a fire burn in your stomach.	*A fyer dir in boyd.*	A *fy*-er dir in boyd.
May a fire catch hold of you.	*A fyer oyf dir.*	A *fy*-er oyf dir.
May a fire consume you. Literally means: A fire is seeking you.	*A fyer zucht din.*	A *fy*-er *zucht* din.
May a fire inflame your liver.	*A fyer in doyn leber.*	A *fy*-er in *doyn leb*-er.
May a red beet grow out of your belly button, and may you pee borsht.	*Zoln dir vaksn burekes fun pupik, in zolst pishn mit borsht.*	*Zoln* dir *vaks*-en bu-*rek*-es fun *pup*-ik in *zolst pish*-en mit *borsht*.
May a soft balcony fall on your head.	*A vecher balkon dir in kop.*	A *vech*-er *bal*-kon dir in *kop*.
May a thunder shake your body.	*A duner dir in dee zaytn arayn.*	A *dun*-er dir in dee *zayt*-en a-rhine.
May a wheel run over your skull.	*A rud zol dir ariber iber dee gehirn.*	A *rud* zol dir a-*rib*-er i-*ber* dee ge-*hirn*.
May all the possible bad dreams stuff your head.	*Ale beyze chlumut tsu dayn kop.*	Ale *beyz*-e *chlum*-ut tsu dayn kop.
May all your teeth fall out, except one to give you a toothache.	*Ale tseyn zoln dir aroysfaln, nor eyner zol dir blaybn – oyf tsonveytik.*	*Al*-e *tsey*-en zoln dir a-*roys*-faln, nor *eyn*-er zol dir *blayb*-en – oyf tson-*vey*-tik.
May an epidemic strike you.	*A mageyfe zol oyf dir kumen.*	A ma-*geyf*-e zol oyf dir kum-en.

English	Yiddish	How You Say It
May calamity strike you.	*Eyn oyschapenysh zol oyf dir kumen.*	Eyn oys-*chap*-ensysh zol oyf dir *kum*-en.
May calamity strike you and your filthy family.	*A brod oyf dir un oyf dyn.*	A *brod* oyf dir un oyf dyn.
May calamity strike you in the stomach [in your head, in your guts].	*A klog dir in boyd [in kop, in dyn podle kishkes].*	A *klog* dir in boyd [in *kop*, in *dyne pod*-le *kishk*-es].
May characters like you be sown thickly and germinate thinly.	*Azoyne zol men kedicht zeyn in seeter zoln zee oyfgeyn.*	A-*zoyne* zol men ke-*dicht zeyn* in *sit*-er zoln zee *oyf*-geyn.
May cholera rot your bones.	*A cholere dir in dee beyner.*	A *chol*-er-e dir in dee *beyn*-er.
May destruction strike you.	*A churbn oyf dir.*	A *churb*-en oyf dir.
May disaster strike you.	*A klog zol dir trefn.*	A *klog* dir *tref*-en.
May doctors know you well and vice versa.	*Doktoyrim zoln visen fun dir un di fun doktoyrim.*	*Dok*-toy-rim zoln *vis*-en fun dir un di fun *dok*-toy-rim.
May God give you a large cancer as well as a small cancer—and then you will have a nice outfit.	*Got zol dir gebn a rak mit a rekele – vestu hobn a gantsn kostium.*	*Got* zol dir *geb*-en a *rak* mit a *rek*-e-le *ves*-tu *gants*-en *kos*-ti-um.

In Yiddish this is a pun. The Yiddish word *rak* is both a term for cancer and a term for jacket.

English	Yiddish	How You Say It
May God see to it that no smoke leaves your chimney for eight consecutive years.	*Got zol gebn em zol dir acht yor nun anand nit geyn keyn royn fun koytn.*	Got zol *geb*-en em zol dir *acht* yor nun a-*nand* nit *geyn keyn royn* fun *koyt*-en.
May I grieve after you.	*A brod zol in nod dir hobn.*	A *brod* zol in *nod* dir.
May I have the privilege of sewing your shroud.	*A soyve zol id dir machn.*	A *soyv*-eh zol id dir *mach*-en.
May I mourn your death.	*Id zol veyn oyf dayne iorn.*	Id zol *veyn* oyf *dayne* i-orn.
May I not lose anything more than your head.	*Mer vi dayn kop zol id nit onvern.*	Mer vi *dayn kop* zol id nit on-*vern*.
May illness strike your brain.	*A chvarobe dir in dee gehern.*	A *chvar*-ob-e dir in dee ge-*her*-en.
May it end badly for you.	*Zol es dir aroys bokem.*	Zol es dir a-*roys bok*-em.
May misfortune fall upon you.	*Eyn umgleek oyf dir.*	Eyn um-*gleek* oyf dir.
May misfortune strike you.	*Eyn umgleek zol dir trefn.*	Eyn um-*gleek* dir tref-en.
May misfortune strike your guts.	*Eyn umgleek dir in kishkes.*	Ryn um-*gleek* dir in *kishk*-es.
May prayers be offered up for your soul.	*Me zol did trogn un zingn.*	Me zol did *trog*-en un *zing*-en.

Literally means: May you be carried away amidst song.

English	Yiddish	How You Say It
May sickness drain all you have and may you pawn your wife's skirt.	*Oyskrenkn zolstu alts vos du farmogst un farzetsn der vaybs spodnitse.*	Oys-*krenk*-en *zols*-tu alts vos du far-*mogst* un far-*zets*-en der *vayb*-es spod-*nit*-se.
May someone call a doctor for you urgently, and when he arrives, they should inform him that it is too late.	*Me zol rufn tsu dir srotshne a dokter un az iener vet kumen zol men im zogn az me darf shoyn nit.*	Me zol *ruf*-en tsu dir *srotsh*-ne a *dok*-ter un az i-*en*-er vet *ku*-men zol men im *zog*-n az me darf *shoyn* nit.
May suffering consume you.	*Oysgefleekt zolstu vern.*	Oys-*gef*-leekt *zols*-tu vern.
May syphilis consume your flesh.	*Frantsn zoln esn dayn dayb.*	*Frants*-en zoln esn *dayn dayb.*
May the Angel of Death fall in love with you.	*Der malechamo'ves zol zid id dir farlibn.*	Der ma-*lech*-a-mo'ves zol zid dir far-*lib*-en.
May the Angel of Death remove you from this world.	*Der malechamo'ves zol did tsunemen fun der velt.*	Der ma-*lech*-a-mo'ves zol did tsu-*nem*-en fun der velt.
May the Devil [the cotton-wool maker] take you.	*Chapt did der ruech [dir vate-macher].*	*Chapt* did der *ru*-ech [dir *va*-te-*ma*-cher].

The "cotton-wool maker" is a popular Yiddish euphemism for the Devil.

English	Yiddish	How You Say It
May the Devil carry you on his shoulders.	*Trogn zol did der ruech oyf di pleytses.*	*Trog*-en zol did der *ru*-ech oyf di *pleyts*-es.
May the devil take your thieving father.	*A ruech in dayn ganvishn tatn arayn.*	A *ru*-ech in dayn gan-*vish*-en *tat*-en a-*rhine*.

English	Yiddish	How You Say It
May the Lord send a blessing for success to your pack of troubles.	*A mazel-bracheh zol dir der eyberster tsores.*	A *maz*-el *brach*-eh zol dir der ey-*best*-er *tsor*-es.
May there be a great fair in Paradise and may you be very successful there.	*Zol shoyn zany a groyser irid in geneden, un zolst dortn matslich shem.*	Zol *shoyn* za-ny a *groys*-er i-*rid* in gen-e-den un zolst *dort*-en *mats*-lich shem.
May trouble come upon your head.	*A brod tsu dayn kop.*	A *brod* tsu *dayn* kop.
May worms hold a wedding in your stomach and invite their relatives from all over.	*Zoln verem praven a chaseneh in dayn boyn in aynladn ale zeyere kroyvim—fun inupets biz sladobke.*	Zoln *ver*-em prav-en a *chas*-e-neh in dayn *boyn* in ayn-*lad*-en ale *zey*-ere *kroy*-vim—fun in-u-*pets* biz *slad*-ob-ke.
May you be a dead duck tonight.	*A kaporeh zolstu veren hayntike nacht.*	A ka-*por*-eh *zols*-tu ver-en *hayn*-ti-ke nacht.
May you be a lamp: hang by day, burn by night and be snuffed out in the morning.	*Zolst syn vee a lump: hengen by tog, brenen by nacht in oysgeyn zolstu in der fri.*	Zolst syn vee a *lump*: *heng*-en by *tog*, bren-en by *nacht* in *osy*-geyn *zols*-tu in der fri.
May you be as tormented in your death as I am in my life.	*Zolst zid azoy matern mitn toyt vee in mater zid.*	Zolst zid a-*zoy* ma-*tern* *mit*-en *toyt* vee in ma-ter zid.
May you be buried nine feet deep in the ground.	*Ver bagrobn nayn eyln in der erd.*	Ver ba-*grog*-en *nayn* *eyl*-en in der erd.
May you be carried out on a dead man's stretcher.	*Trogn zol men dir oyf der miteh.*	*Trog*-en zol men dir oyf der *mit*-eh.

English	Yiddish	How You Say It
May you be consumed by fire.	*A fyer zol dir farbrenen.*	A *fy*-er zol dir far-*bren*-en.
May you be consumed by syphilis and may your nose drop off.	*Frantsn zoln dir oyf esn un din noz zol dir aropfaln.*	*Frants*-en zoln dir oyf esn un din *noz* zol dir a-*rop*-fal-en.
May you be healthy and tough as iron, so much so that you cannot bend over.	*Nezunt un shtark zolstu zayn vee ayzn, zolst zid nit kenen.*	Ne-*zunt* un *shtark* zols-tu zayn vee *ayz*-en *zolst* zid nit *ken*-en.
May you be in mourning in summer days and suffer from a toothache on winter nights.	*In dee zumerdike teg zolstu zitsen shiveh un in dee vinterdike necht zolstu zid rayst oyf dee teyn.*	In dee zu-*mer*-di-ke teg *zols*-tu *zits*-en *shi*-veh un in dee vin-*ter*-di-ke nect *zols*-tu zid rayst oyf dee *teyn*.
May you be invited to a feast by the governor and may you belch in his face.	*Me zol din aynladn tsum gubernator oyf a seydeh in du zolst im gebn a grepts in ponem arayn.*	Me zol din ayn-*lad*-en gu-*ber*-na-tor oyf *sey*-deh in du zolst im gebn a *grepts* in *pon*-em a-rhine.
May you be spared the indignities and illnesses of old age.	*Zolst farshporn di bizoynut un di krenh fun der elter.*	*Zolst* far-*shpor*-en di bi-*zoyn*-ut un *kren*-eh fun der elt-er.
May you be struck dumb forever.	*Antshvign zolstu vern oyf eybik.*	Ant-*shvig*-en *zols*-tu vern oyf ey-*bik*.
May you become so rich that your widow's husband should never have any worries about his livelihood.	*Zolst vern azoy rayd almo'nes man zol zid keyn mol nit zorgen vegn perno'se.*	Zolst vern a-*zoy rayd* almo'nes man zol zid *keyn* mol nit *zorg*-en *veg*-en.

English	Yiddish	How You Say It

| May you break all your bones. | *Tseboyechen zolstu ruk-un-lend.* | Tse-*boy*-ech-en *zols*-tu *ruk*-un-lend. |

Literally means: May you break your back and your sides.

| May you break down and collapse. | *Ayngebrochen zolstu vern.* | Aynge-*broch*-en *zols*-tu vern. |

| May you break your arms and your legs. | *Oysbrechen zolstu dee hent mit dee fus.* | Oys-*brech*-en *zols*-tu dee *hent* mit dee *foos*. |

| May you choke on a fish dumpling. | *A feshkneydh zol zid dir shtelnin haldz.* | A fesh-*kneyd*-eh zol zid dir *shtel*-nin *haldz*. |

| May you choke on your next bite of your food. | *Dershtikt zolstu vern mit bisn.* | Der-*shtikt zols*-tu vern mit bis-en. |

| May you choke on your next juicy morsel. | *Dershtikt zolstu dir mit dem fatn bisn.* | Der-*shtikt zols*-tu dir mit dem *fat*-en bis-en. |

| May you enjoy your wedding breakfast and choke on your last bite. | *Zolst hobn hano'ie fun dayn chuneh-seudeh un zid dervargn mit letstn bisn.* | *Zolst hob*-en ha-*no*'ie fun *dayn chun*-eh *seu*-deh un zid der-*varg*-en mit *letst*-en *bis*-en. |

| May you explode— from pleasure. | *Platsn zolstu—fun naches.* | *Plats*-en *zols*-tu—fun *nach*-es. |

| May you fall and never rise up. | *aln zolstu nit oyfshteyn.* | *Fal*-en *zols*-tu ni oyf-*shteyn*. |

| May you feel pricks, bites, aching bones and sores all over your body. | *S'zol dir onchapn a shtechenish un a brechenish, a raysenish un a baysenish.* | S'zol dir on-*chap*-en a *shtech*-en-ish un a *brech*-en-ish, a *ryas*-en-ish una *bays*-en-ish. |

English	Yiddish	How You Say It
May you go begging from door to door with your descendants for many generations.	*Iber di hyzer zolstu zid shlepn mit kindskinder oyf dur-durut.*	I-ber di hy-*zer zols*-tu zid *shlep*-en mi kinds-*kind*-er oyf dur-*dur*-ut.
May you go crazy and run around the streets.	*Meshugeh zolstu vern un orumloyfn iber dee gasn.*	Me-*shug*-eh *zols*-tu vern un o-*rum*-loyf-en i-ber dee gas-en.
May you have a long bout of bad luck.	*A biter mazel oyf dir.*	A bi-ter *maz*-el oyf dir.
May you have a revolution in your stomach.	*S'zol dir dreyn in boyd.*	S'*zol* dir *drey*-en in boyd.
May you have terrible stabbing pains in your bowels.	*S'zol dir shnaydn bay di kishkes.*	S'zol dir *shnayd*-en bay di keesh-kes.
May you have the juiciest goose—but no teeth; the best wine—but no sense of taste; the most beautiful wife—but be impotent.	*Zolst hobn di same fete gandz—nor kit keyn tseyner; di beste vayn nor nit keyn chushtem; di senste vayb—nor nit keyn zehrut.*	Zolst *hob*-en di sa-me fete gandz—nor kit *key*-en *tseyn*-er di *bes*-te *vine* nor nit *keyn chush*-tem di *sens*-te *vayb*—nor nit *key*-en *zeh*-rut.
May you live until one hundred and twenty—with a wooden head and glass eyes.	*Zolst lebn biz hoondert un tsvantseek yor—mit a heeltsernem kop in glezerne oygn.*	Zolst *leb*-en biz *hoond*-ert un *tsvants*-eek yor—mit a heel-tser-nem kop in glez-erne oyg-en.
May you never be remembered.	*Nit gedacht zolstu vern.*	Nit ge-*dacht zols*-tu vern.
May you never become old.	*Nit derlebn zolstu eltertsu vern.*	Nit der-*leb*-en *zols*-tu el-*ter*-tsu vern.

English	Yiddish	How You Say It
May you never enjoy any goodness in your home.	*Nit hobn zolstu keyn guts in stub.*	Nit *hob*-en *zols*-tu *key*-en guts in *stub.*
May you never have anything good all your life.	*Nit hobn zolstu keyn guts vayl du lebst.*	Nit *hob*-en *zols*-tu *key*-en guts *vayl* lebst.
May you not stand in a cemetery, only lie there.	*Oyf keyn guten-ort zolstu nit shteyn nor lign.*	Oyf *keyn gut*-en-ort *zols*-tu nit *shtey*-en nor *lig*-en
May you own ten ships full of gold and may you spend it all on your illnesses.	*Tsen shifn mit gold zolstu farmogn in dos gantse gelt zolstu farkrenkn.*	Tsen *shif*-en mit gold *zols*-tu far-*mog*-en in do *gant*-se *gelt zols*-tu far-*krenk*-en.
May you push up daisies soon.	*Groz zol oyf dir vaksn.*	Groz zol oyf dir *vaks*-en.
May you romp with the Angel of Death.	*Mitn malechamo'ves zolstu zid shpeln.*	*Mit*-en ma-*lech*-a-mo'ves *zols*-tu zid *shpel*-en.
May you rot so badly that goats, skunks and pigs will decline to travel in the same cart as you.	*Zolst azoy farfoylt vern az tsign, tchoyrn, un chazirim zoln zid opzogn tsu forn mit dir in eyn fur.*	Zolst a-*zoy* far-foylt vern az *tsign, tchoy*-ern un cha-*zir*-im zoln zid op-*zog*-en tsu *forn* mit dir in eyn *fur.*
May you run to the toilet every three minutes or every three months.	*Loyn zolstu in bet-chakis iede dray minut oder iede dray chadoshim.*	*Loyn zols*-tu in bet-*chak*-is i-ed-e *dray min*-ut o-*der* i-ed-e *dray cha*-do-shim.
May you speak so eloquently that only a cat will understand you.	*Zolst azoy seyn redn az nor di kats zoln dir farshteyn.*	Zolst a-*zoy sey*-en *red*-en az nor *kats* zoln dir *farsht*-eyn.

English	Yiddish	How You Say It
May you spend all your money on doctors.	*Farkrenk dos oyf dayn guf.*	Far-*krenk* dos oyf *dayn* guf.

Literally means: May you spend all your money on your body.

May you suffer a cruel and unusual death.	*A miteh-meshuneh zolstu hobn.*	A *mit*-eh-me-*shun*-eh *zols*-tu *hob*-en.
May you turn into a pancake and be snatched away by the cat.	*Vern zol fun dir a blintshik in dee kats zol did chapn.*	*Vern* zol fun dir a *blint*-shik in de *kats* zol di chapn.
May you turn into a pancake and he into a cat. He should eat you and choke on you— that way we will be rid of both of you.	*Vern zol fun dir a blintshik in fun is a kats. Er sol dir oyfesn un mit dir zin dervargn—volt men fun ayn beydn ptur gevorn.*	*Vern* zol fun dir a *blint*-shik in fun is a *kats*. Er sol dir *oyf*-esn un mit dir zin der-*varg*-en— *volt* men fun ayn *beyd*-en *ptur* ge-vorn.
May your arms and hands be paralyzed.	*Opkenumen zoln dir dee hent vern.*	Op-*ken*-u-men zoln dir dee *hent vern.*
May your bones rot in hell.	*Dayne beyner zoln foylen in gehnum.*	Dayne *beyn*-er zoln *foyl*-en in geh-*num*.
May your enemies sprain their ankles dancing on your grave.	*Zoln dayne shunim oyslenkn zeyere fim ven zey veln tantsn oyf dayn keyver.*	Zoln *day*-ne *shun*-im oys-*len*-ken *zey*-ere fim ven zey *veln tants*-en oyf dayn *key*-ver.
May your father be possessed by a demon.	*A ruech in dayn tatn arayn.*	A *ru*-ech in dayn *tat*-en a-rhine.
May your grandfather be possessed by a demon.	*A ruech in dayn zeydn arayn.*	A *ru*-ech in dayn *zeyd*-en a-*rhine*.

English	Yiddish	How You Say It
May your guts come out.	*Dee kishkes zoln dir aroym.*	Dee *keesh*-kes zoln dir a-*roym.*
May your guts freeze so hard that only hellfire will be able to thaw them.	*Zoln dayn kishkes farfrayrn vern oyf azoy fil, az nor der fyer fun gehnum zol zey kenen tseshmeltsn.*	Zoln *dayn kish*-kes far-*frayr*-en vern oyf a-*zoy* fil, az nor der *fy*-er fun *geh*-num zol zey *ken*-en tsesh-*melt*-sen.
May your innards turn and grind so much, people will think you are an organ grinder.	*Sazol dir azoy dreyen boyd me zol meynen az sayiz a katerinke.*	Sa-zol dir a-zoy *drey*-en *boyd* me zol *mey*-nen az *say*-iz a ka-*ter*-in-ke.
May your intestines be pulled out of your belly and wound around your neck.	*Aroysshlepn zol men dir dee kishkes fun boyd un arumviklen zee ebern haldz.*	A-*roys*-shlep-en zol men dir dee *keesh*-kes fun *boyd* un a-*rum*-vik-len zee e-*bern haldz.*
May your legs be lopped from under you.	*Dee fim zoln dir untergehakt vern*	Dee fim *zoln* dir un-ter-*gehakt vern.*
May your liver come out through your nose piece by piece.	*Dee leber zol dir shteklechvayz doord der noz aroysfleen.*	Dee LEB-er dir shtek-*lech*-vayz doord der noz a-*roys*-fleen.
May your luck light your way for you like the waning moon at the end of the month.	*Dyn mazel zol dir laychtn vee dee levone in sof.*	Dyn *maz*-el zol dir *laycht*-en vee dee *lev*-one in sof.
May your soul enter a cat and may a dog bite it.	*Dyn neshome zol arayngeyn in a kats, un a hoont zol er a bis tun.*	Dyn ne-*shom*-e zol a-*rhine*-geyn in a kats un a *hoont* zol er a bis tun.

English	Yiddish	How You Say It

Mensch   *Mensch*   *Mensch*

Someone who does good work and helps others is called a *mensch*. Literally it means: person or human being. Use this word when you want to give others the impression that someone is truly worthy of respect for his good deeds, would make a good husband or business partner, treats others fairly and meets his obligations.

Mess   *Mishmash*   Mish-*mash*

When everything is a mess, you can call it a "*mishmash*." Also fits when you think something is a hodgepodge or a jumble. It is believed this comes from the fifteenth century and was formed by a repetition of the word *mash*.

Mixed-up person   *Farmisht*   Far-*misht*

When you think someone is all mixed-up or confused, you can say, "You're *farmisht*."

Money buys everything except brains.	*Far gelt bakumt men alts, nor kain saychel nit.*	Far gelt *bak*-umt men alts, nor *kain say*-chel nit.
Money causes conceit and conceit leads to sin.	*Gelt brengt tsu ga'aveh un ga'aveh tsu zind.*	Gelt *brengt* tsu ga'a-veh un ga'a-veh tsu zind.
Money goes to money.	*Gelt gayt tsu gelt.*	Gelt *gayt* tsu gelt.
Money is round; it rolls away from you.	*Gelt is keylechdik; amol iz es do, amol iz es dort.*	Gelt is key-*lich*-dik; a-*mol* iz es do, a-*mol* iz es dort.
Money lost, nothing lost; courage lost everything lost.	*Gelt farloren, gor nit farloren; mut farloren, alts farloren.*	Gelt far-*lor*-en, gor nit far-*lor*-en; mut far-*lor*-en, alts far-lor-en.
My money went down the drain.	*In drerd meyn geytl.*	In *drerd* meyn *geyt*-el.

English	Yiddish	How You Say It

Nerve   *Chutzpah*   *Chuts*-pah
Audacity. Means a lot of nerve. This can be a good thing or bad thing. When you use it positively it means someone has a lot of nerve and daring. But negatively it can mean someone has a lot of nerve and has gone too far. This word has its origins in the Hebrew word *huspa,* which means to be insolent.

Nosh   *Nash or nashn*   *Nash*
Light snack or light meal. This comes from the Yiddish word *nash* or *nashn,* which means to eat sweets or to nibble on food. Its origins can be found in the Middle High German word *naschen,* which means to nibble.

Nudge   *Nudjen*   *Nud*-jen
Pester or bore. Someone who pesters, annoys or complains persistently. Its origins are from the Polish word *nudzi,* which means the same.

Nudnik   *Nudnik*   *Nood*-nik
If someone is badgering you and they are a very annoying person, you can call them a *nudnik.* Also used when someone is a bore, being obnoxious, nagging you or generally being a nuisance.

Oh, God   *Gottenyu*   *Got*-ten-yu
Use it to express despair, anguish or to show pity for something. It's a substitute for "Oh, God!"

Oh, hell! or Damn it!   *A broch!*   Ah *brooch*

Oh, no.   *Oy vay.*   *Oy* vay.
Oy vay means Oh, no, but in Yiddish actually means Oh, woe. People also use it to say things like "How terrible" or "That's horrible."

Old wives' tale   *Bubbeh meisseh*   *Bub*-eh *my*-seh
Use it when you think someone is telling you an old wives' tale or something completely unbelievable. It literally means a grand-mother's story, but don't use it around your grandmother if she knows Yiddish, or she'll be pretty angry. It's usually used when you just don't believe what someone is telling you.

English	Yiddish	How You Say It
On summer days he should mourn, and on wintry nights, he should torture himself.	*In dee zumerdike teg zol er zitsn shiveh, un in dee vinterdike necht zich raysn ayf di tseyn.*	In dee zu-*mer*-dike teg zol er *zitsn* shiveh, un in di vin-*ter*-dike *necht* zich *rays*-en ayf di tsey-en.
One lie is a lie, two are lies, but three is politics.	*Ayner iz a ligen, tsvai iz ligens, dray iz politik.*	Ay-*ner* iz a *lig*-en, *tsvai* iz *lig*-ens, *dray* iz pol-*it*-ik.
One misfortune is too few for him.	*Eyn umgleek az far im veynik.*	Eyn um-*gleek* az far im *vey*-nik.
Onions should grow on your navel.	*Zol dir vaksn tzibbeles fun pupik.*	Zol dir *vox*-en *tzib*-eh-les fun *poop*-ik.

| Panhandler | *Shnorrer* | *Shnor*-er |

Also can refer to a beggar, moocher or freeloader. *Shnorrers* make a career of panhandling and think they are doing others a favor by allowing them to do a *mitzvah* (good deed) through donating to the needy.

| Piece of shit | *Shtik drek* | *Shtick* drek |

| Pig | *Chazzer* | *Chaz*-er |

Also someone who is greedy, eats too much or takes more than his share.

| Pimp | *Yentzer* | *Yents*-er |

Also, someone who will screw you in a nonsexual way.

| Pitiable person | *Nebach* | *Neb*-ach |

| Poor dresser | *Shlump* | *Shloomp* |

Also unstylish or with bad posture. When a someone corrects another because his shoulders are drooping, they can say "Don't *shlump!*"

English	Yiddish	How You Say It
Poverty is no disgrace, but also no great honor	*Orem iz nit kayn shand, ober oych kayn groisser koved nit.*	O-*rem* iz nit *kayn* shand, o-*ber* oych *kayn* grois-er *kov*-ed nit.

Put up or shut up.   *Toches ahfen tish.*   *Too*-ches ah-fin tish.
    Also can be used to mean: "Let's conclude this!" Or "Come clean, buddy!" Literally means: Put your buttocks on the table.

Rich men are often lean and poor men are fat.	*Faran dareh gvirim un feteh oremeleyt.*	*Far*-an *dar*-eh ge-*vir*-im un *fet*-eh o-rem-el-eyt.

Rugelach   *Rugelach*   Ru-*ge*-lach
    Crescent-shaped cookie made from a cream-cheese dough filled with jam, chocolate, cinnamon, sugar or nuts, or some combination of these ingredients, cut into a triangle and rolled up.

Run away from an insult but don't chase after honor.	*Far umkoved antloyf, ober yog zich nit noch koved.*	*Far* um-*kov*-ed ant-*loyf*, o-ber *yog* zich nit *noch* ko-ved.

Scatterbrain   *Draikop*   *Dray*-kop
    Also someone who goes all out trying to confuse you. Often this refers to a con artist who deliberately is trying to take advantage of you.

Schmear   *Schmir*   *Schmear*
    To use a dab of cream cheese is one common meaning, but you will also hear *shmeer* used when people talk about buying a bunch of things together, such as "She bought the whole *shmear*." The Yiddish word *schmir* means smear or smudge from the word *shmirn* or grease, which stems from the Middle High German word *smiren* also meaning to smear or grease. When not used in the context of eating, shmear can mean the whole works or to be excessively kind for selfish gains.

English	Yiddish	How You Say It

Schmooze   *Shmuesn*   *Shmues*-en
   Engage in casual conversation many times in order to gain an
   advantage or make a social connection. The Yiddish word *shmuesn*
   has its origins both in *shmues* (chat) or *schmue* (rumor).

Self-made fool   *Shmuck*   *Shmuck*
   Also dickhead, idiot or jerk. Another word for penis.
   Literally means: Jewel.

Shame   *Shandeh*   *Shan*-deh
   Use when you are embarrassed about something or think something
   is a shame.

She should have   *Shteyner zol zi hoben,*   *Shtey*-ner zol zi *hob*-en,
stones and not   *nit kayn kinder.*   nit *kayn kin*-der.
children.

Shit head   *Kucker*   *Kuck*-er

Shit on a stick   *Drek oyf a shpendel*   *Drek* oyf a *shpen*-del
   Also means: As unimportant as dung on a piece of wood.

Shlep   *Shlepn*   *Shlep*-en
   Means to drag an object with difficulty. It can also be used to mean a
   long, tedious or difficult journey. Like Wasn't that trip to the city a
   shlep? Its origin is the German word *schleppen,* which means to drag.

Shlock joint   *Shlak*   *Shlak*
   Junk shop or has no value. Literally it means evil. When you go into
   a store that sells cheap stuff, you can call it a "*shlok* joint." Its origin
   is the Middle High German word *slag.*

Shmo   *Shmok*   *Shmok*
   If you think someone is a complete jerk or patsy, you can call him a
   shmo. It comes from the Yiddish word, *shmok,* which means penis or
   fool.

English	Yiddish	How You Say It

Shnook   *Shnook*   *Shnook*
When someone is easily victimized, in other words stupid, a sucker or a dupe, you can call them a *shnook*. Its origins are in the Lithuanian word *snukis*, which means mug or snout.

Shnoz   *Shnoits*   Shnoyts
Nose, which comes from the Yiddish word *shnoits*, which means snout.

Shove it up your ass.   *Shtup es in toches.*   *Shtoop* es in *too*-ches.

Shut your mouth.   *Farmach dos moy.*   Far-*mach* dos *moyl.*

Slob   *Zhlob*   *Zhlob*
Also someone who is clumsy, uncouth or foolish.

Smelly person   *Shtinker*   *Shtink*-er
Also can refer to someone who behaves offensively.

So it goes in this world: one has the purse, the other has the money.   *Azoy gayt ayf der velt: ayner hot di beytel, der tsvayter hot di gelt.*   A-*zoy gayt* ayf der velt: *ayn*-er hot di *beyt*-el, der *tsvayt*-er hot di gelt

So what do you think you can do to me? Nothing.   *Ti mir eppes.*   Tee mir *ep*-is.

Sponger   *Shlepper*   *Shlep*-per
Also can refer to someone who always tags along or a jerk.

Stones on his bones.   *Shteyner ayf zayne bainer.*   *Shteyn*-er ayf *zayne bain*-er.

Sucker   *Shlumpf*   *Shlumpf*
Also a patsy, fall guy or second-rater.

English	Yiddish	How You Say It
Ten ships of gold should be his and the money should only make him sick.	*Tsen shifn mit gold zol er farmorgn, un dos gantse gelt zol er farkrenkn.*	Tsen *shif*-en mit gold zol er far-*morg*-en un does *gant*-se getl zol er far-*krenk*-en.
The first time it's smart, the second time it's cute, the third time you get a sock in the teeth.	*Ain mol a saichel, dos tsvaliteh mol chain, dem dritten mol git men in di tsain.*	Ain mol a sai-*chel*, dos tsva-*lit*-eh mol *chain*, dem *drit*-ten mol git men in di tsain.
The heaviest burden is an empty pocket.	*Der shversteh ol iz a laydikeh kesheneh.*	Der *shverst*-eh ol iz a *layd*-ik-eh *kesh*-en-eh.
The poor man's enemies are few, the rich man's friends are even fewer.	*Der oreman hot vainik eint, der reicher hot vainiker freint.*	Der *ore*-man hot *vain*-ik, der *reich*-er hot *vain*-ik-er freint.
They should free a madman, and lock him up.	*A meshugener zol men oyshrabn, un im arayn shrabn.*	A me-*shug*-en-er zol men oy-*shrab*-en, un im a-*rhine* shrab-en.
Thief	*Gonif*	*Gon*-if

Also can be used to refer to someone who is a swindler, crook, burglar or racketeer.

English	Yiddish	How You Say It
Those who can't bite should not show their teeth.	*Az men ken nit beissen, zol men nit veizen di tsayin.*	az men ken nit *beis*-en zol men nit *veiz*-en di *tsayn*
Throw salt in his eyes, pepper in his nose.	*Zalts im in di oygen, feffer im in di noz.*	*Zalts* im in di *oyg*-en, *fef*-er im in di *noz*.
To hell with him.	*Ich hob im in bod.*	Ich *hob* im in bod.

Literally means: I have him in the bath house.

English	Yiddish	How You Say It
To hell with it.	*Zole es brennen.*	Zol es *Bren*-in.

Tough luck   Tough *toches*   *Too*-ches

Literally means tough ass. Use when you want to say tough luck or too bad. *Toches* is another word for butt, ass, backside or fanny. You get the idea.

Trashy   *Drek*   *Drek*

Also can be used to refer to someone who is cheap, trashy, shoddy, worthless or useless.

Troubles   *Tsores*   *Sor*-es

When you have a lot of problems or troubles, you can say you are facing a lot of *tsores*. Also can be used to express misery.

Truth   *Emmes*   *Em*-mes

Truth, or on the level. If you want to indicate that you believe something someone is telling you, you say that it's "*emmes*."

Unkosher   *Traif*   *Trayf*

Forbidden food and not prepared by the rules of Jewish dietary laws. It's the opposite of kosher. You may hear this word also used for non-food items, such as books or movies, that are forbidden. For example, "Don't go to see *Deep Throat* [a pornographic flick]—it's *traif.*"

Venereal disease   *Fransn zol esn zayn*   *Frans*-en zol esn zayn
should consume his   *layb.*   layb.
body.

Weakling   *Nebbish*   *Neb*-ish

Also a pitiable person but not as bad as a *Nebach*.

What's new?   *Nu?*   Nu?

Nu is a commonly used Yiddish slang for "What's new?" but has many other uses as well. It can also be used as a question, such as "*Nu*? When does he show up?"; to show impatience, such as "*Nu!* What was said?"; to dare someone, "*Nu*, prove it to me!"; or to just make a strong statement, "*Nu*, I told you so!"

English	Yiddish	How You Say It
When a mother shouts at her child "Bastard," you can believe her.	*Az di muter shrayt oyfen kind "Mamzer," meg men ir gloiben.*	Az di mu-*ter shrayt* oyf-en *kind* "Mam-zer," meg men ir *gloib*-en.
When does a wealthy man go hungry? When the doctor orders him.	*Ven hungert a nogid? Ven der doktor hayst im.*	Ven *hung*-ert a *nog*-d? Ven der *dokt*-or *hayst* im.
When the head is a fool, the whole body can go to hell.	*Az der kop iz a nar, ligt der gantser guf in der erd.*	Az der *kop* iz a *nar, ligt* der *gants*-er guf in der erd.
When the stomach is empty, so is the brain.	*Az der mogen iz laidik iz der moi'ech oich laidik.*	Az der *mog*-en iz *laid*-ik iz der *moi*'ech oich laid-ik.
When you grease the palm, everything goes easy.	*Az me shmirt, fort men.*	Az me *shmirt,* fort men.
When you sow money, you reap fools.	*Az me zayt gelt, vaksn naronim.*	Az me *zayt* gelt, *vaks*-en na-ron-im.
Who are you kidding, who do you think you are screwing around with?	*Vemen barestu?*	*Vay*-men *bar*-es-tu?

Literally means: Who are you screwing?

Who is smart? He whose fortune follows him.	*Der iz klug? Vos zeyn mazel gayt im noch.*	Der iz *klug*? Vos zeyn *maz*-el *gayt* im *noch.*
Why bother getting up alive?	*Farshporn zol er oyf tsu shteyn?*	*Farsh*-porn zol er oyf tsu shteyn?
Wise	*Saichel*	*Say*-chel

When you think someone is very smart or wise, you say they have *saichel.* This can also mean someone has common sense, tact or diplomacy.

English	Yiddish	How You Say It
With a good guest, you are happy when he arrives; with a bad one, when he leaves.	*Mit a gutn gast frayt men zich ven er kumt arayn; mit a shlechtn gast, ven er gayt avek.*	Mit a gu-TEN gast *frayt* men zich ven er *kumt* a-*rhine*; mit a *shlecht-* en gast, ven er *gayt* a-*vek.*
Worms eat you up when dead and worries eat you up alive.	*Verem essn toiterhayt un deiges lebedikerhayt.*	Ve-*rem* es-sen toi-*ter-* hayt un *dei-*ges le-*bed-* i-ker-hayt.
You ass.	*Chamoyer du einer.*	Cha-*moy-*er du *eye-*ner.
Also can mean: You dope, You idiot.		
You can vomit from this.	*Me ken brechen fun dem.*	Me *ken brech-*en fun dem.
You cannot pay a debt with a noble pedigree.	*Mit zechus oves batsolt men nit kayn choyves.*	Mit *zach-*us oves *bat-*solt men nit *kayn choy-* ves.
You don't scare me.	*Gai strasheh di gens.*	Gay stra-sheh di gens.
Literally means: Go scare the geese.		
You moron.	*Chamoyer du ainer.*	Cha-moy-er du *ain-*er.
You should choke on it.	*Der shtikt zolst du veren.*	Der *shtikt* zolst du *ver-* en.
You should explode.	*Gai plotz.*	Gay plotz!
Also can mean: Go split your guts!		
You should get a stomach cramp.	*Zol dir grihmen in boych.*	Zol dir *grih-*men in boych.
You should have no better luck.	*Keyn besern mazel zolstu.*	Key-en *bes-*ern *maz-*el *zols-*tu.

English	Yiddish	How You Say It
You should only get a stomach cramp.	*Zol dich chappen beim boych.*	Zol dich *chap*-in byme boych.
You should shove it up your ass.	*Zolst es shtupin in toches arayn.*	Zolst es *shtoop*-en in *too*-ches a-rhine.
You should swell up like a mountain.	*Zolst geshvolln veren vi a barg.*	Zolst geh-*shvol*-en ver-en vi a barg.
You're nuts.	*Bist tsedrayt.*	Bist tse-*drayt*.
You're nuts.	*Bist meshugeh.*	Bist me-*shug*-eh.
You're pissing in the wind.	*Gai feifen ahfen yam.*	Gay *fife*-en *ah*-fin yam.

Literally means: Go whistle on the wind.

Your stomach will rumble so badly, you'll think it was a Purim noisemaker.	*Es zol dir dunern in boych, vestu meyen az s'iz a homon klaper.*	Es zol dir *dun*-ern in boych, *ves*-tu *mey*-en az s'iz a *hom*-on *klap*-er.

For those not familiar with the holiday of Purim: As part of the celebration, various kinds of noisemakers are used to drown out the name of the enemy of the Jews—Haman—as the story of Esther is told during the reading of the *Megillah*, which is the Book of Esther.

Yiddish
to English
Glossary

Yiddish	How You Say It	English
A beyn zol dir in haldz blayben shtekn.	A *beyn* zol dir in *haldz blayb*-en *shtek*-en.	May a bone remain stuck in your throat.
A biter mazel oyf dir.	A bi-*ter maz*-el oyf dir.	May you have a long bout of bad luck.
A brand dir in dee kishkes.	A *brand* dir in dee *keesh*-kes.	May a fire burn in your guts.
A broch!	Ah *brooch!*	Oh, hell! or Damn it!
A brod oyf dir un oyf dyn.	A *brod* oyf dir un oyf dyn.	May calamity strike you and your filthy family.
A brod tsu dayn kop.	A *brod* tsu dayn kop.	May trouble come upon your head.
A brod zol in nod dir hobn.	A *brod* zol in nod dir.	May I grieve after you.
A cholere dir in dee beyner.	A *chol*-er-e dir in dee *beyn*-er.	May cholera rot your bones.
A choleryeh oyf dir.	A cho-*ley*-er-yeh oyf dir.	A plague on you.
A churbn oyf dir.	A *churb*-en oyf dir.	May destruction strike you.

Yiddish	How You Say It	English
A chvarobe dir in dee gehern.	A *chvar*-ob-e dir in dee ge-*her*-en.	May illness strike your brain.
A duner dir in dee zaytn arayn.	A *dun*-er dir in dee *zayt*-en a-rhine.	May a thunder shake your body.
A feshkneydh zol zid dir shtelnin haldz.	A fesh-*kneyd*-eh zol zid dir *shtel*-nin haldz.	May you choke on a fish dumpling.
A finsteren sof.	A *fin*-ster-en sof.	A horrible end should befall you.

Also can mean: May there be a dark ending for you.

A finsteren yor.	A *fin*-ster-en yor.	A plague on you.

Literally means: A year (for dark on you).

A freint bekamt men umzist; a soineh muz men zich koifn.	A *freint bek*-amt men um-*zist*; a *soi*-neh muz men zich *koif*-en.	A friend you can get for nothing: an enemy has to be bought.
A freint darf men zich koifn; sonem kright men umzist.	A *freint* darf men zich *koif*-en; *son*-em *kright* men um-zist.	A friend you have to buy; enemies you get for nothing.
A fyer dir in boyd.	A *fy*-er dir in *boyd*.	May a fire burn in your stomach.
A fyer in doyn leber.	A *fy*-er in *doyn leb*-er.	May a fire inflame your liver.
A fyer oyf dir.	A fy-er oyf dir.	May a fire catch hold of you.
A fyer zol did farbrenen.	A *fy*-er zol did far-*bren*-en.	May you be consumed by fire.
A fyer zol did trefn vee du redst.	A *fy*-er did *tref*-en vee du *redst*.	A fire should strike you while you are speaking now.

Yiddish	How You Say It	English
A fyer zol im trefn.	A *fy*-er zol im *tref*-en.	He should burn up.
A fyer zucht din.	A *fy*-er *zucht* din.	May a fire consume you.
Literally means: A fire is seeking you.		
A gehenem oif im.	A geh-*hen*-em oyf im.	He should go to hell.
A geshvir iz a gutch zach bei yenem unhern orem.	A *gesh*-vir iz a *gutch* zach bei *yen*-em un-hern o-*rem*.	A boil is fine as long as it's under someone else's arm.
A groys gesheft zol er hobn mit shroyre: vus er hot, zol men bay im nit fregn, un vos men fregt zol er nisht hobn.	A *groys* ge-*sheft* zol er *hob*-en mit *shroy*-re: vus er hot, zol men bay im nit *freg*-en, un vos men *fregt* zol er nisht hob-en.	He should have a large store; and whatever people ask for he shouldn't have, and what he does have shouldn't be requested.
A harmat zol dayn kop tseshmetern.	A *harm*-at zol *dayn kop* tsesh-met-ern.	May a cannon ball split your skull.
A hiltsener tsung zol er bakumn.	A hil-*tsen*-er zol er ba-kumn.	He should grow a wooden tongue.
A kaporeh zolstu veren hayntike nacht.	A ka-*por*-eh *zols*-tu ver-en hayn-ti-ke.	May you be a dead duck tonight.
A kleyn kind zol noch im heysn.	A *kleyn* kind zol *noch* im heys-en.	A young child should be named after him.
A klog dir in boyd [in kop, in dyn podle kiskes].	A *klog* dir in *boyd* [in kop, in *dyne* pod-le kisk-es].	May calamity strike you in the stomach [in your head; in your guts].
A klog zol dir trefn.	A *klog* dir *tref*-en.	May disaster strike you.

Yiddish	How You Say It	English
A kluger vaist vos er zogt, a nar zogt vos er vaist.	A *klug*-er *vaist* vos er zogt, a *nar* zogt vos er vaist.	A wise man knows what he says, a fool says what he knows.
A kramp dir in boyd.	A *kramp* dir in boyd.	A cramp in your stomach.
A kramp im in layb [in boyach; in di kishkes; in di gederem, in di finger].	A *kramp* in *layb* [in *boy*-ach; in di keesh-kes, in di *ged*-er-em, in di *fing*-er].	A cramp in his body [in his stomach; in his guts; in his bowels; in his fingers and toes].
A krenk zol im arayn in di yosles.	A *krenk* zolim a-*rhine* in dee yos-lis.	May a disease enter his gums.
A magaifeh zol dich trefen.	A ma-*gay*-feh *zol* dich tref-en.	A plague should befall you.
A mageyfe zol oyf dir kumen.	A ma-*geyf*-e zol oyf dir kum-en.	May an epidemic strike you.
A mazel-bracheh zol dir der eyberster tsores.	A *maz*-el *brach*-eh zol dir der ey-*best*-er tsor-es.	May the Lord send a blessing for success to your pack of troubles.
A meshugener zol men oyshrabn, un im arayn shrabn.	A me-*shug*-en-er zol men oy-*shrab*-en, un im a-*rhine* shrab-en.	They should free a madman, and lock him up.
A miteh-meshuneh zolstu hobn.	A *mit*-eh-me-*shun*-eh *zols*-tu hob-en.	May you suffer a cruel and unusual death.
A ruech in dein tatn's tateh.	A *ru*-ech in dein *tat*-en's *ta*-teh.	Go to the devil.
A ruech in dein tatn's tatenarein.	A *ru*-ech in dein *tat*-en's *tat*-en-a-*Rhine*.	Go to the devil.

Yiddish	How You Say It	English
A rud zol dir ariber iber dee gehirn.	A *rud* zol dir a-*rib*-er i-*ber* dee ge-hirn.	May a wheel run over your skull.
A ruech in dayn ganvishn tatn arayn.	A *ru*-ech in dayn gan-*vish*-en *tat*-en a-*rhine.*	May the devil take your thieving father.
A ruech in dayn tatn arayn.	A *ru*-ech in dayn *tat*-en a-*rhine.*	May your father be possessed by a demon.
A ruech in dayn tatns tatn arayn.	A *ru*-ech in dayn *tat*-ens tatn a-*rhine.*	May a demon take your father's father.
A ruech in dayn zeydn arayn.	A *ru*-ech in dayn *zeyd*-en a-*rhine.*	May your grandfather be possessed by a demon.
A shnaydenish dir in boyd.	A *shnay*-de-nish dir in boyd.	A stabbing pain in your stomach.
A shtrek dir oyfn haldz.	A *shtrek* dir oyf-en haldz.	A rope around your neck.
A shvartz yor.	A *shvartz* yor.	A black year.
A soyve zol id dir machn.	A *soyv*-eh zol id dir *mach*-en.	May I have the privilege of sewing your shroud.
A vecher balkon dir in kop.	A *vech*-er *bal*-kon dir in kop.	May a soft balcony fall on your head.
A zisn toyt zolstu hobn a trok mit tsuker zoldid iberforn.	A *zis*-en *toyt zols*-tu *hob*-en a trok mit *tsuk*-er *zol*-did i-ber-forn.	I wish you a sweet death: a truck full of sugar should run over you.

Yiddish	How You Say It	English
Ain mol a saichel, dos tsvaliteh mol chain, dem dritten mol git men in di tsain.	Ain mol a sai-*chel* dos tsva-*lit*-eh mol *chain,* dem *drit*-ten mol git men in di tsain.	The first time it's smart, the second time it's cute, the third time you get a sock in the teeth.
Ale beyze chlumut tsu dayn kop.	Ale *beyz*-e *chlum*-ut tsu dayn kop.	May all the possible bad dreams stuff your head.
Ale tseyn zoln bay im aroysfalen, not eyner zol im blayben oyf tsonveytung.	Al-e *tseyn zoln* bay im a-*roys*-fal-en not *eyn*-er zol in *blayb*-en oyf tson-*veyt*-ung.	All his teeth should fall out except one to make him suffer.
Ale tseyn zoln dir aroysfalen, nor eyner zol dir blaybn—oyf tsonveytik.	*Al*-e *Tsey*-en zoln dir a-roys-falen, nor *eyn*-er zol dir *blayb*-en—oyf tson-*vey*-tik.	May all your teeth fall out, except one to give you a toothache.
Ale tsores (vos id hob oyf mayn hartn) zoln oysgeyn tsu dayn kop.	Ale *tsor*-es (vos id *hob* oyf *mayn hart*-en) zoln osy-*gey*-en tsu *dayn kop.*	All the troubles (that weigh down my heart) should fall on your head.
Ale tsores vos ich hob oyf mayn hartsn, zoln oysgeyn tsu zayn kop.	*Ale tsor*-es vos ich hob oyf *may*-en *harts*-en, zoln *oysg*-eyn tsu *zhine* kop.	All problems I have in my heart should go to his head.
Aleh tsores oyf zein kop.	Al-eh *tsor*-es oyf zine kop.	He should have lots of trouble.
Alter kucker Also means: Old fogy. Literally means: An old defecator.	Al-ter kuck-er	Lecherous old man

Yiddish	How You Say It	English
Antshvign zolstu vern oyf eybik.	Ant-*shvig*-en *zols*-tu vern oyf ey-bik.	May you be struck dumb forever.
Aroysshlepn zol men dir dee kishkes fun boyd un arumviklen zee ebern haldz.	A-*roys*-shlep-en zol men dir dee *keesh*-kes fun *boyd* un a-rum-vik-len zee e-bern haldz.	May your intestines be pulled out of your belly and wound around your neck.
Ayner iz a ligen, tsvai iz ligens, dray iz politik.	Ay-ner iz a *lig*-en, *tsvai* iz *lig*-ens, dray iz pol-*it*-ik.	One lie is a lie, two are lies, but three is politics.
Ayngebrochen zolstu vern.	Aynge-*broch*-en *zols*-tu vern.	May you break down and collapse.
Az der kop iz a nar, ligt der gantser guf in der erd.	Az der *kop* iz a *nar, ligt* der *gants*-er guf in der erd.	When the head is a fool, the whole body can go to hell.
Az der mogen iz laidik iz der moi'ech oich laidik.	Az der *mog*-en iz *laid*-ik iz der *moi*'ech oich laid-ik.	When the stomach is empty, so is the brain.
Az di muter shrayt oyfen kind: "Mamzer," meg men ir gloiben.	Az di mu-ter shrayt oyf-en *kind*: "*Mam*-zer," meg men ir *gloib*-en.	When a mother shouts at her child: "Bastard," you can believe her.
Az me hot gelt, iz men klug un shain un men ken gut zingn.	*Az me hot gelt, iz men* Klug *un* shain *un men* ken *gut Zing*-en.	If you have money, you are wise and good-looking and can sing well too.
Az me laight arayn kadoches, nemt men aroyz a krenik.	Az me laight a-*rhine* ka-*doch*-es, nemt men a-*royz* a *kren*-ik.	If you invest in a fever, you will realize a disease.
Az me lebt mit a tayvel, vert men a tayvel.	Az me *lebt* mit a *tayv*-el, vert men a *tayv*-el.	He who lives with the devil, becomes a devil.

Yiddish	How You Say It	English
Az me lozt a chazzer aruf af'n bank, viler af'n tish.	Az me lozt a *chazz*-er a-ruf af'n *bank* vil-er af'n *tish.*	Give a pig a chair, he'll want to get on the table.
Az me redt, derredt men zich.	Az me redt, *der*-redt men zich.	If you keep on talking, you will end up saying what you didn't intend to say.
Az me shloft mit hint shtayt men oyf mit flay.	Az me shloft mit *hint, shtayt* men oyf mit *flay.*	If you lie down with the dogs, you get up with the fleas.
Az me shmirt, fort men.	Az me *shmirt,* fort men.	When you grease the palm, everything goes easy.
Az me shport nit dem groshn, hot men nit dem rubel.	Az me *shport* nit dem *grosh*-en, hot men nit dem *rub*-el.	If you don't save the penny, you'll not have the dollar.
Az me shvaygt iz men a halber nar; az me redt iz men a gantser nar.	Az me *shvagt* iz men a *halb*-er nar; az me *redt* iz men a *gants*-er nar.	He who keeps quiet is half a fool; he who talks is a complete fool.
Az me tut zich lodn, kumt men sey vi nit tsum shodn.	Az me tut zich *lod*-en, kumt men sey vi nit tsum *shod*-en.	From litigation you can never recover your loss.
Az me vil nit alt verren, zol men zich yungerhayt oyfhengen.	Az me vil nit alt *ver*-en zol, men zich yun-*ger*-hayt oyf-*heng*-en.	If you want to avoid old age, hang yourself in youth.
Az me zayt gelt, vaksn naronim.	Az me *zayt* gelt, *vaks*-en na-*ron*-im.	When you sow money, you reap fools.

Yiddish	How You Say It	English
Az men chazert tsu fil iber vi grecht men iz, vert men umgerecht.	Az men *chaz*-ert tsu fil i-ber vi *grecht* men iz, vert men um-ger-echt.	If you repeat often enough that you're right, you will discover you are wrong.
Az men ganvet a sach ayer, ken men oich verren a nogid.	Az men *gan*-vet a *sach* ay-er, *ken* men *oich* ver-ren a *nog*-id.	If one steals a lot of eggs, one can also become rich.
Az men hot di matbayeh, hot men di dayeh.	Az men hot di mat-*bay*-eh, hot men di *day*-eh.	If you have the money, you have the say.
Az men iz biz tsvantsik yor a kind, iz men tsu ayn-un-tsvantsik a behaymeh.	Az men iz biz *tsvant*-sik yor a *kind*, iz men tsu ayn un *tsvant*-sik a be-*hay*-meh.	If you're a child at twenty, you're an ass at twenty-one.
Az men ken nit beissen, zol men nit veizen di tsain.	Az men ken nit *beis*-en zol men nit *veiz*-en di *tsain*.	Those who can't bite should not show their teeth.
Az men krigt zich mitn rov, muz men sholem zeyn mitn shainker.	Az men *krigt* zich *mit*-en rov, muz men *shol*-en zyen *mit*-en *shaink*-er.	If you're at odds with your rabbi, make peace with your bartender.
Azoy fil ritzinoyl zol er oystrinkn	A-*zoy* fil rit-*zin*-oyl zol er oy-*strink*-en.	He should drink too much castor oil.
Azoy gayt ayf der velt: ayner hot di beytel, der tsvayter hot di gelt.	A-*zoy gayt* ayf der velt: *ayn*-er hot di *beyt*-el der *tsvayt*-er hot di gelt.	So it goes in this world: one has the purse the other has the money.
Azoyne zol men kedicht zeyn in seeter zoln zee oyfgeyn	A-*zoyne* zol men ke-*dicht zeyn* in *sit*-er zoln zee *oyf*-geyn.	May characters like you be sown thickly and germinate thinly.

Yiddish	How You Say It	English

Bareh nit. *Bar-*eh nit. Don't fuck with me.

Also means: Don't fornicate around, but more mildly can mean Don't
fool around, don't annoy or don't bother someone.

Beser a krumer fus   *Bes-*er a *krum-*er fus   Better a crooked foot
ayder a krumer kop.   ay-*der* a *krum-*er *kop.*   than a crooked mind.

Beser dos kind zol   *Bes-*er dos kind *zol*   Better to do nothing
vaynen ayder der foter.   *vayn-*en ay-*der* der *fot-*   than to make
   er.   something into
     nothing.

Beser volt oyf dyn ort a   *Be-*ser volt oyf dyn *ort*   It would have been
shteyn arayn.   a *shtey-*en a-*rhine.*   better if a stone had
     come out of your
     mother's womb, rather
     than you.

Beygl   *Bay-*gul   Bagel

Probably one of the most popular Jewish foods that has found its
way into many American hearts. It's a hard, ring-shaped bread roll
that finds its origins in the Middle High German word *bougel.*

Bialy   Bee-*ya-*lee   Bialy

Roll, shaped like a disc, which is thicker around the outer edges and
flattened in the middle. The middle of a *bialy* is traditionally filled
with onion pieces and sometimes cheese. It gets its name from the
Polish city Bialystok, which is credited with its creation.

Bist meshugeh.   Bist me-*shug-*eh.   You're nuts.

Bist tsedrayt.   Bist tse-*drayt.*   You're nuts.

Blintse   *Blint-*seh   Blintz

Looks like a thick crepe or thin pancake that's folded around some
type of filling. Cheese, potatoes and fruit, individually or combined,
are the most common fillings used. Its origin is in the Russian word
blinets or "little pancake."

Yiddish	How You Say It	English

Bubbeh meisseh   *Bub*-eh *my*-seh   old wives' tale
Use it when you think someone is telling you an old wives' tale or something completely unbelievable. It literally means a grandmother's story, but don't use it around your grandmother if she knows Yiddish, or she'll be pretty angry. It's usually used when you just don't believe what someone is telling you.

Bulvan   *Bul*-van   Impolite person
Also means: A rude or ill-mannered person.

Chamoyer du ainer.   Cha-*moy*-er du *ain*-er.   You moron.

Chamoyer du einer.   Cha-*moy*-er du *eye*-ner.   You ass.
Also can mean: You dope, you idiot.

Chapt did der ruech   *Chapt* did der *ru*-ech   May the Devil [the
[dir vate-mache]   [dir *va*-te-*ma*-cher].   cotton-wool maker] take you.
The "cotton-wool maker" is a popular Yiddish euphemism for the Devil.

Chazzer   *Chaz*-er   Pig
Also someone who is greedy, eats too much or takes more than his share.

Chepeh zich nit tsu   *Chep*-eh zich nit tsu   Don't bother me.
mir.   meer.
Literally means: Don't attach yourself to me!

Chepeh zich op fun   *Chep*-eh zich *op* fun   Don't bother me.
mir.   meer.

Chepeh zich op fun   *Chep*-eh zich op fun   Leave me alone.
mir.   meer.
Also means: Get away from me!

Yiddish	How You Say It	English
Chutzpah	*Chuts*-pah	Nerve

Audacity. Means a lot of nerve. This can be a good thing or bad thing. When you use it positively, it means someone has a lot of nerve and daring. But negatively it can mean someone has a lot of nerve and has gone too far. This word has its origin in the Hebrew word *huspa*, which means to be insolent.

Yiddish	How You Say It	English
Cock zich oys.	*Cock* zich oys.	Go take a shit.

Also means: Go take a shit for yourself.

Yiddish	How You Say It	English
Dayne beyner zoln foylen in gehnum.	Dayne *beyn*-er zoln *foyl*-en in geh-*num*.	May your bones rot in hell.
Dee fim zoln dir untergehakt vern.	Dee fim *zoln* dir un-ter-*gehakt* vern.	May your legs be lopped from under you.
Dee kishkes zoln dir aroym.	Dee *keesh*-kes zoln dir a-roym.	May your guts come out.
Dee leber zol dir shteklechvayz doord der noz aroysfleen.	Dee *leb*-er dir shtek-*lech*-vayz doord der noz a-*roys*-fleen.	May your liver come out through your nose piece by piece.
Der iz klug? Vos zeyn mazel gayt im noch.	Der iz *klug*? Vos zeyn *maz*-el *gayt* im *noch*.	Who is smart? He whose fortune follows him.
Der lebn iz di gresteh metsi'eh—me wrigt es umzist.	Der *leb*-en iz di *grest*-eh met-si'eh—me *wrigt* es um-*zist*.	Life is the biggest bargain—we get it for nothing.
Der malechamo'ves zol did tsunemen fun der velt.	Der ma-*lech*-a-mo'ves zol did tsu-*nem*-en fun der *velt*.	May the Angel of Death remove you from this world.
Der malechamo'ves zol zid id dir farlibn.	Der me-*lech*-a-mo'ves zol zid dir far-*lib*-en.	May the Angel of Death fall in love with you.

Yiddish	How You Say It	English
Der mazel macht klug, veil der mazel macht reich.	Der *maz*-el macht *klug*, veil der *maz*-el macht *reich*.	Fortune makes you smart, because fortune makes you rich.
Der oreman hot vainik eint, der reicher hot vainiker freint.	Der *ore*-man hot *vain*-ik, der *reich*-er hot *vain*-ik-er *freint*.	The poor man's enemies are few, the rich man's friends are even fewer.
Der shtikt zolst du veren.	Der *shtikt* zolst du *ver*-en.	You should choke on it.
Der shversteh ol iz a laydikeh kesheneh.	Der *shverst*-eh ol iz a *layd*-ik-eh *kesh*-en-eh.	The heaviest burden is an empty pocket.
Dershtikt zolstu dir mit dem fatn bisn.	Der-*shtikt* *zols*-tu dir mit dem *fat*-en bis-en.	May you choke on your next juicy morsel.
Dershtikt zolstu vern mit bisn.	Der-*shtikt* *zols*-tu vern mit bis-en.	May you choke on your next bite on your food.
Doktoyrim zoln vesen fun dir un di fun doktoyrim.	*Dok*-toy-rim zoln *ves*-en fun dir un di fun *dok*-toy-rim.	May doctors know you well and vice versa.
Drai mir nit kain kop.	Dray meer nit *kayn* kop.	Don't bother me.

Literally means: Don't twist my head.

Draikop	*Dray*-kop	Scatterbrain

Also someone who goes all out trying to confuse you. Often this refers to a con artist who deliberately is trying to take advantage of you.

Drek	*Drek*	Trashy

Also can be used to refer to someone who is cheap, trashy, shoddy, worthless or useless.

Yiddish	How You Say It	English

Drek oif a shpendel   *Drek* oyf a *shpen*-del   Shit on a stick
Also means: As unimportant as dung on a piece of wood.

Dumkop   *Dum*-kop   Dumbbell or dunce
Literally means: Dumb head

Dyn mazel zol dir   Dyn *maz*-el zol dir   May your luck light
laychtn vee dee levone   *laycht*-en vee dee *lev*-   your way for you like
in sof.   one in sof.   the waning moon at
     the end of the month.

Dyn neshome zol   Dyn ne-*shom*-e zol a-   May your soul enter
arayngeyn in a kats,   *rhine*-geyn in a *kats* un   a cat and may a dog
un a hoont zol er a   a *hoont* zol er a bis   bite it.
bis tun.   tun.

Emmes   *Em*-mes   Truth
Truth, or on the level. If you want to indicate that you believe
something someone is telling you, you say that it's *emmes*.

Er redt zich eyn a   Er *redt* zich eyn a   He talks himself into
krenk.   *krenk.*   sickness.

Er zol ainemen a   Er zol ai-*ne*-men a   He should have lots of
miesseh meshuneh.   *mies*-eh *mesh*-un-eh.   trouble.

Er zol altsting zen, un   *Er zol* als-*ting zen, un*   He should see
nit hobn farvos (mit   nit hob-*en far-vos (mit*   everything, but have
vos) tsu koyfn.   *vos)* tsu *koyf*-en.   no reason (with which)
     to buy it.

Er zol einemen a   Er *zol ein*-eh-men a   He should go to hell.
meeseh meshuneh.   *meese*-eh meh-*shun-eh.*

Er zol einemen a   Er zol ein-*em*-en a   He should go to hell.
miesseh meshuneh.   mies-eh me-*shun*-eh
Literally means: He should meet a strange death.

Yiddish	How You Say It	English
Er zol gayn in drerd.	Er zol *gayn* in drerd.	He should go to hell.
Er zol kakn mit blit un mit ayter.	Er zol *kak*-en mit *blit* un mit *ayt*-er.	He should crap blood and pus.
Er zol vaksen vi a tsibeleh, mit dem kop in drerd.	Er zol *vak*-s-en a *tsib*-el-eh, mit dem *kop* in drerd.	He should grow like an onion with his head in the ground.
Er zol zain ayf tsores.	Eer zol *zain* ayf *tsor*-es.	He should have lots of trouble.
Es hart mich vi di vant.	Es *hart* mich vee dee *vant.*	I don't give a damn.

Literally means: It bothers me like a wall.

Yiddish	How You Say It	English
Es vet helfn vi a toitn bahnekes.	Es vet *helf*-en vee a *toyt*-en bahn-kis.	It's useless, it'll help like bloodletting on a dead body.
Es zol dir dunern in boych, vestu meyen az s'iz a homon klaper.	Es zol dir *dun*-ern in boych, *ves*-tu *mey*-en az s'iz a *hom*-on *klap*-er.	Your stomach will rumble so badly, you'll think it was Purim noisemaker.

For those not familiar with the holiday of Purim, as part of the celebration various kinds of noisemakers are used to drown out the name of the enemy of the Jews—Haman—as the story of Esther is told during the reading of the *Megillah*, which is the Book of Esther.

Yiddish	How You Say It	English
Eyn umgleek oyf dir.	Eyn um-*gleek* oyf dir.	May misfortune fall upon you.
Eyn oyschapenysh zol oyf dir kumen.	Eyn oys-*chap*-ensysh zol oyf dir *kum*-en.	May calamity strike you.
Eyn umgleek az far im veynik.	Eyn um-*gleek* az far im *vey*-nik.	One misfortune is too few for him.

Yiddish	How You Say It	English
Eyn umgleek dir in kishkes.	Ryn um-*gleek* dir in *kishk*-es.	May misfortune strike your guts.
Eyn umgleek zol dir trefn.	Eyn um-*gleek* dir *tref*-en.	May misfortune strike you.
Farcockt	Far-*cocked*	Full of shit

Shitty or badly soiled. When you think someone is full of shit, you can say, "You're *farcockt.*"

Faln zolstu nit oyfshteyn.	*Fal*-en *zols*-tu ni oyf-shteyn.	May you fall and never rise up.
Far der klenster toyveh vert men a ba'al-choyv.	Far der *klenst*-er *toyv*-eh vert men a ba'al-choyv.	For the smallest favor you become a debtor.
Far gelt bakumt men alts, nor kain saychel nit.	Far gelt *bak*-umt men alts, nor *kain say*-chel nit.	Money buys everything except brains.
Far umkoved antloyf, ober yog zich nit noch koved.	*Far* um-*kov*-ed ant-*loyf*, o-ber *yog* zich nit *noch* ko-*ved.*	Run away from an insult but don't chase after honor.
Faran dareh gvirim un feteh oremeleyt.	*Far*-an *dar*-eh ge-*vir*-im un *fet*-eh o-rem-el-eyt.	Rich men are often lean and poor men are fat.
Farblondjet	Far-*blond*-jet	Confused person

When you think someone is totally confused, you can say they are *farblondjet.* Also used when you think someone is lost.

Fardrai zich dem kop.	Far-*dray* zich dem kop.	Go screw up your head.
Fardray zich dayn aygenem kop.	Far-*dray* zich *dayn* ay-gen-em kop.	Go drive yourself crazy.

Yiddish	How You Say It	English
Farkrenk dos oyf dayn guf.	Far-*krenk* dos oyf *dayn* guf.	May you spend all your money on doctors

Literally means: May you spend all your money on your body.

Farloreneh yoren iz erger vi a farloreneh gelt.	Far-*lor*-en-eh *yor*-en iz *erg*-er vi a far-*lor*-en-eh gelt.	Lost years are worse than lost dollars.

Farmach dos moyl.	Far-*mach* dos *moyl.*	Shut your mouth.

Farmisht	Far-*misht*	Mixed-up person

When you think someone is all mixed-up or confused, you can say, "You're *farmisht.*"

Farshporn zol er oyf tsu shteyn?	*Farsh*-porn zol er oyf tsu shteyn?	Why bother getting up alive?

Feh	*Fay*	Fooey

Multipurpose word that can mean "Fooey!"; "That's terrible!"; "I hate that!"; "That stinks!"; or "How disgusting!"

Finstere leyd zol nor di mama oyf im zen.	Fin-*ster*-eh leyd zol nor di *ma*-ma oyf im zen.	Black sorrow is all that his mother should see of him.

Foiler	*Foy*-ler	Lazy man

Folg mich a gang un gai in drerd.	*Folg* mich a *gang* un *gay* in drerd.	Do me a favor and drop dead.

Fransn zol esn zayn layb.	*Frans*-en zol esn *zayn* layb.	Venereal disease should consume his body.

Frantsn zoln dir oyf esn un din noz zol dir aropfaln	*Frants*-en zoln dir oyf esn un din *noz* zol dir a-*rop*-fal-en.	May you be consumed by syphilis and may your nose drop off.

Yiddish	How You Say It	English
Frantsn zoln esn dayn dayb.	*Frants*-en zoln esn dayn dayb.	May syphilis consume your flesh.
Fun glik tsum umglik iz a shpan; fun umglik tsum glik iz a shtik veg.	Fun *glik* tsum um-*glik* iz a *shpan*; fun um-*glik* iz a shtik veg.	From fortune to misfortune is a short step; from misfortune to fortune is a long way.
Fun iberessn cholyet men mer vi fun nit deressn.	Fun i-*ber*-es-sen *chol*-yet men mer vi fun nit *der*-es-sen.	From overeating one suffers more than from not eating enough.
Gai bareh di vantsen.	*Gay bar*-eh di *vant*-sen.	Go bother the bedbugs.
Gai cocken ahfen yam.	Gay *cock*-en ah-fin yam.	Go shit on the ocean.

Also can be used to mean: Don't bother me, or Get lost.

Yiddish	How You Say It	English
Gai fardrai zich dein aigenem kop.	*Gay far*-dray *zich dine* eye-gen-em *kop.*	Drive yourself crazy.
Gai fardrai zich deyn kop.	*Gay far*-dray zich *deyn kop.*	Go drive yourself crazy.
Gai fardray zich dayn aigenem kop.	*Gay* far-*dray* zich *dayn* ay-*gen*-em.	Go mix yourself up, not me.
Gai feifen ahfen yam.	Gay *fife*-en *ah*-fin yam.	You're pissing in the wind.

Literally means: Go whistle on the wind.

Yiddish	How You Say It	English
Gai in drerd arayn.	*Gay* in *draird* a-*rhine.*	Go to hell.

Literally means: Go down into the earthly grave!

Yiddish	How You Say It	English
Gai kab enyeh mattereh.	Gay kab *en*-yeh ma-ter-eh.	Go to hell.

Yiddish	How You Say It	English
Gai kabenyeh matyreh.	*Gay* ka-*ben*-yeh ma-*tyr*-eh.	Go to hell.
Gai klop zich kop in vant.	*Gay klop* zich *kop* in vant.	Go bang your head against the wall.
Gai plotz. Also can mean: Go split your guts.	*Gay plotz.*	You should explode.
Gai strasheh di gens. Literally means: Go scare the geese.	*Gay stra*-sheh di *gens.*	You don't scare me.
Gai tren zich.	Gay tren zich.	Go fuck yourself.
Gai tsebrech a fus.	*Gay* tse-*brech* a foos.	Go break a leg.

Gefilte   Ge-*fil*-te.   Gefilte fish

Stuffed fish. Made using a whole fish, then chopping the fish meat into very small pieces. Most often, carp, pike or salmon is used and sometimes a mixture of more than one of these types of fish. Other common ingredients include onions, celery, carrots, sugar, white pepper, salt, eggs and matzo meal. The mixture is then stuffed back into the fish's skin or body cavity (bones and all) and boiled or baked. Today most people just buy balls of gefilte fish mixture in jars or cans, and you will find it on the dinner table at all Jewish holiday celebrations.

Geharget zolstu veren. Literally means: You should get killed.	Geh-*har*-get *zolst*-u *ver*-en.	Drop dead.
Gelt brengt tsu ga'aveh un ga'aveh tsu zind.	Gelt *brengt* tsu ga'a-veh un ga'a-veh tsu zind.	Money causes conceit and conceit leads to sin.
Gelt farloren, gor nit farloren; mut farloren, alts farloren.	Gelt far-*lor*-en, gor nit far-*lor*-en; mut far-*lor*-en, alts far-lor-en.	Money lost, nothing lost; courage lost everything lost.

Yiddish	How You Say It	English
Gelt gayt tsu gelt.	Gelt *gayt* tsu gelt.	Money goes to money.
Gelt is keylechdik; amol iz es do, amol iz es dort.	Gelt is key-*lich*-dik; a-*mol* iz es do, a-*mol* iz es dort.	Money is round, it rolls away from you.
Gelt tsu fardinen iz gringer vi tsu haltn.	Gelt tsu far-*din*-en iz *gring*-er vi tsu halt-en.	It's easier to earn money than to keep it.
Gey in drerd mit dee beyner.	Gey in *drerd* mit dee *beyn*-er.	Go to hell together with your bones.
Gey tsu al dee gute-ior!	Gey tsu al dee *gut*-e-ior.	Go to hell.

Literally means: Go to all the demons.

| *Gey tsum shvare-ior.* | *Gey* tsum *shvar*-eh-i-or. | Go to the black pit. |
| *Gezunt-heit.* | Ge-*zunt*-heit. | Good health. |

Commonly used when someone sneezes, sometimes in conjunction with "God bless you." You can also use it as part of a toast.

| *Gonif* | *Gon*-if | Thief |

Also can be used to refer to someone who is a swindler, crook, burglar or racketeer.

| *Got helft dem oreman; er farhit im fun tey'ereh avayres.* | *Got* helft dem o-*re*-man; er *far*-hit im fun tey'er-eh a-*vayr*-es. | God helps the poor man; he protects him from expensive sins. |
| *Got zol dir bentshn mit dray mentshn: eyner zol did haltn, der tsveyter zol did shpaltn un der driter zold id bahaltn.* | *Got* zol dir *bent*-shen mit dray *ment*-shin: ey-ner zol did *halt*-en, der *tsveyt*-er zol di *shpalt*-en un der *drit*-er zold id ba-halt-en. | God should bless you with three persons: one should hold you; the second should kill you and the third should bury you. |

Yiddish	How You Say It	English
Got zol dir gebn a rak mit a rekele—vestu hobn a gantsn kostium.	*Got* zol dir *geb-en* a rak mit a *rek-e-le—ves-*tu *gants-*en kos-ti-um.	May God give you a large cancer as well as a small cancer—and then you will have a nice outfit.

In Yiddish this is a pun. The Yiddish word *rak* is both a term for cancer and a term for jacket.

Got zol dir hedfen dee zolstu altsdeng, zen un nit hobn far vos tsu koyfn.	Got zol dir *hed-*fen dee *zols-*tu alts-deng, zen un nit *hob-*en far vos tsu *koyf-*en.	God should help you to see everything and not have the where-withal to buy anything.
Got zol gebn em zol dir acht yor nun anand nit geyn keyn royn fun koytn.	Got zol *geb-*en em zol dir *acht* yor nun a-*nand* nit *geyn keyn royn* fun *koyt-*en.	May God see to it that no smoke leaves your chimney for eight consecutive years.
Got zol gebn, er zol hobn altsding vos zayn harts glist, nor er zol zayn geleymt oyf ale ayvers un nit kenen rirn mit der tsun.	*Got* zol *geb-*en er zol hob-en *alts-*ding vos zhine *harts glist*, nor er zol *zayn* ge-*leymt* oyf ale ay-vers un nit *ken-*en rirn mit der *tsun*.	God should bestow him with everything his heart desires, but he should be a quadriplegic and not be able to use his tongue.
Got zol oyf im onshikn fin di tsen makes di beste.	*Got* zol oyf im on-*shik-*en fun di *tsen mak-*es di *bes-*te.	God should visit upon him the best of the Ten Plagues.
Gottenyu	*Got-*ten-yu	Oh, God

Use it to express despair, anguish or to show pity for something. It's a substitute for "Oh, God!"

Groisser gehilleh.	*Groys-*eh geh-*hill-*eh.	Big deal, so what.
Groisser gornisht.	*Groys-*er *gor-*nisht.	Big good-for-nothing.

Yiddish	How You Say It	English

Groisser putz   *Groys*-er putz   Big idiot
    Also: Big prick, big penis, big fool or big shot.

Groz zol oyf dir vaksn.   Groz zol oyf dir *vaks*-   May you push up
                             en.   daisies soon.

Gut zol oyf im onshikn   Gut *zol oyf in* onsh-*ikn*   God should visit upon
fin di tsen makes di   *fin di tsen* mak-*es di*   him the best of the
beste.   bes-*te.*   Ten Plagues.

Hak mir nit kain   *Hak* meer nit *kayn*   Don't bother me.
cheinik.   *chy*-nik.
    Literally means: Don't bang on the teakettle.

Halvah   Hal-*vah*   Halvah
    Sweetmeat. Claimed not only by the Jews, but many Middle Eastern
    cultures. It originated in the Balkans and eastern Mediterranean
    regions. It's made with sesame seeds and honey or sugar syrup.
    Other ingredients can be added, such as dried fruit, pistachio nuts
    and almonds. Some people add cinnamon and cardamom. The
    ingredients are blended together, heated and poured into bars or
    loaves. In addition to the Yiddish word *halvah*, Turkish call it *helva*,
    Greeks call it *halva*, Arabs call it *halwa* or *halawi*. In each case it
    translates to "sweetmeat."

Heng dich oyf a   *Heng* dich oyf a tsi-*ker*-   Hang yourself with a
tsikershtrikl vestu hobn   shtrikl *ves*-tu *hob*-en a   sugar rope and you'll
a zisn toyt.   *zis*-en *toyt.*   have a sweet death.

Hindert hayzer zol er   *Hind*-ert hay-zer zol er   A hundred houses
hobn, in yeder hoyz a   *hob*-en, in yed-er hoyz   shall he have; in every
hindert tsimern, in   a *hind*-ert *tsim*-ern, in   house a hundred
yeder tsimer tsvonsik   yed-er *tsim*-er *tsvon*-sik rooms and in every
betn un kadukhes zol   bet-en un ka-*duch*-es   room twenty beds, and
im varfn fin eyn bet in   zol im *varf*-en fin eyn   a delirious fever
der tsveyter.   bet in der tsveyt-er.   should drive him from
                                                          bed to bed.

Yiddish	How You Say It	English
Iber di hyzer zolstu zid slepn mit kindskinder oyf dur-durut.	I-ber di hy-*zer zols*-tu zid *slep*-en mi kinds-*kind*-er oyf dur-dur-ut.	May you go begging from door to door with your descendants for many generations.
Ich cock ahf im.	Ich *cock* ahf im.	I shit on him.
Ich darf es vi a loch in kop.	Ich *darf* es vee a *loch* in kop.	I need it like a hole in the head.
Ich darf es vi a lung un leber oif der noz.	Ich *darf* es vee *lung* un *leb*-er der noz.	I need it like a wart on my nose.
Ich fief oyf dir.	Ich *fife* oyf deer.	I despise you.

Literally means: I whistle on you.

Ich hob dich in bod.	Ich *hob* dich in bod.	Go drown.

Literally: I have you in the bath.

Ich hob dich in drerd.	Ich *hob* dich in draird.	Go to hell.
Ich hob dich in drerd.	*Ich* hob dich in *drerd*!	Go to hell.
Ich hob dich.	Ich hob dich!	Drop dead.
Ich hob im in bod.	Ich *hob* im in *bod*.	To hell with him.

Literally means: I have him in the bath house

Ich hob im in toches.	Ich *hob* im in *too*-ches.	I've got him by the ass.

Also can mean: I have him in my ass.

Id tsu dir oyf simchut, du tsu mir oyf kuliem	Id tsu dir oyf sim-*chut*, du tsu mir oy ku-*li*-em.	I hope I can come to you on joyous occasions and that you will come to me on crutches.

Yiddish	How You Say It	English
Id vel did bagrobn in der erd vi an oytser.	Id vel did ba-*grob*-en in der erd vi an *oyts*-er.	I will bury you in the ground as though you were a treasure.
Id zol did zen oyf eyn fus un du mid mit eyn oyg.	Id zol did *zen* oyf eyn *fus* un du *mid* mit eyn *oyg.*	I hope to see you on one leg and may you see me with one eye.
Id zol hobn a zchut bay got, er zol did tsunenen fun der erd.	Id zol *hob*-en a *zhcut* bay Got, er zol did tsu-*nem*-en fun der erd.	I hope to see you dead.

Literally means: May God grant me the favor of removing you from this world.

Id zol veyn oyf dayne iorn.	Id zol *veyn* oyf *dayne* i-orn.	May I mourn your death.
In dee zumerdike tig zolstu zitsen shiveh un in dee vinterdike necht zolstu zid rayst oyf dee seyn	In dee zu-*mer*-di-ke tig *zols*-tu *zits*-en *shi*-veh un in dee vin-*ter*-di-ke nect *zols*-tu zid rayst oyf dee *seyn.*	May you be in mourning in summer days and suffer from a toothache on winter nights.
In di zumerdike teg zol er zitsn shive, un in di vinterdike necht zich raysn ayf di tseyn.	In di zu-*mer*-di-ke teg zol er *zitsn* shive, un in di vin-*ter*-dike *necht* zich rays-en ayf di *tsey*-en.	On summer days he should mourn, and on wintry nights, he should torture himself.
In drerd meyn geytl.	In *drerd* meyn geyt-el.	My money went down the drain.
In drerd mitten kop.	In *drerd mit*-en kop.	Go to hell!

Literally means: Be in the ground up to your head.

Kaiser	*Kai*-ser	Kaiser roll

Breakfast roll that is light and fluffy on the inside with a thin outer crust. It's made by using a square piece of dough and folding the corners of the dough into the center. Sometimes it's made with

Yiddish	How You Say It	English

poppy seeds and sometimes without the seeds. The name for this roll actually comes from Germany, called *Kaisersemmel* for the German emperor, plus *semmel*, which means roll.

| *Keyn besern mazel zolstu.* | *Key-en bes-ern maz-el zols-tu.* | You should have no better luck. |
| *Khasene hobn zol er mit di malech hamoves tochter.* | *Khas-en-eh hob-en zol er mit di ma-lech ha-mov-es tocht-er.* | He should marry the daughter of the Angel of Death. |

Kibbitz or Kibbitzer *Kib-itz or kib-itz-er* Kibbitz or Kibbitzer
When someone talks too much or gets involved in a subject when they shouldn't, they're called a *kibbitzer*. *Kibbitz* usually means unsolicited or unwanted advice. A person that offers that advice is a *kibbitzer*, also known as a meddlesome spectator.

Klutz *Klutz* Clumsy person
Also a stupid person or a dolt

Knish K-nish Knish
Piece of dough stuffed with potato, meat or cheese and baked or fried, commonly eaten as a snack or an appetizer. Its origins are in the Ukrainian word *Knysh*.

Kosher *Ko-sher* Kosher
Conforming to dietary laws, when talking about food. Its origin is Hebrew and means "fitting" or "proper." Today as slang it's used for nonfood items and means that the material is legitimate, permissible, genuine or authentic. For example, it's commonly used in phrases such as: "Using bikes on the path is *kosher*," or "The story about New York is *kosher*."

Koved *Ko-vid* Honor
When you hold high respect for someone or something, you are said to *koved* it. *Koved* means respect, honor, revere or hold in high esteem.

Yiddish	How You Say It	English
Kucker	Kuck-er	Shit head

Kugel   *Ku*-gel   Kugel

Casserole-like dish made with noodles or potatoes then baked with eggs and seasoning. A sweet kugel can be made with noodles, raisins and apples. In Yiddish *Kugel* actually means ball, which related to its puffed-up or mound shape. The word originates in Middle High German.

Kush in toches arayn.   Kush in too-ches a-   Kiss my ass.
                           rhine.

Kush mich in toches.   Kush mich in too-ches.   Kiss my ass.

Kvell   K-vell   Gloat

Used when you are gloating over your children to show pride in their accomplishments. Someone might also *kvell* when they are enjoying an enemy's bad luck.

Kvetcher   *Kvetch*-er   Complainer

Also can refer to someone who is a whiner. Nothing is ever good enough for them. Rodney Dangerfield was known as the king of the *Kvetchers*. *Kvetch* in Yiddish means to squeeze.

Laks   *Laks*   Lox

Smoked salmon, from the Yiddish word *laks*, which means salmon. This actually comes from the German word for salmon, *lachs*, which was taken from an Indo-European word meaning salmon.

Leyg zin in drerd   Leyg zin in *drerd* a-   Go bury yourself.
arayn.   *rhine.*

Lign drerd un bak   *Lig*-en *drerd* un bak   Go to hell and bake
beygel.   beyg-el.   bagels there.

Literally means: Live underground and bake bagels there.

Ligner   *Lig*-ner   Liar

Loch in kop   Loch in kop   Hole in the head

Yiddish	How You Say It	English
Loy yitslach	Loy *yits*-lach	Incompetent person

Also can refer to someone who has perpetual bad luck.

Loyn zolstu in bet-	*Loyn zols*-tu in bet-	May you run to the
chakis iede dray minut	*chak*-is i-ed-e *dray min-*	toilet every three
oder iede dray	ut o-*der* i-ed-e *dray*	minutes or every three
chadoshim.	*cha*-do-shim.	months.

| *Loz mich tzu ru.* | *Loz* mich tzu *ru.* | Leave me alone. |

Literally means: Let me be in peace.

| *Luftmensh* | *Luft*-mensh | Dreamer |

Also can refer to someone who is an unrealistic optimist; builds castles in the air and has no trade or income. You definitely don't want to loan money to a person like this for their next big scheme to make money. Literally means: Air man.

| *Mamzer* | *Mamz*-er | Bastard |

Also someone who is a nasty, unworthy person.

| *Maven* | *May*-vin | Expert |

When you think someone is an expert, you can call him a *maven.* Also used to indicate someone is an authority on a subject or a connoisseur.

| *Mazel tov.* | *Ma*-zel tov. | Good luck. |

Mazel means luck and *Tov* means good. Also used to say Congratulations!

| *Me ken brechen fun* | Me *ken brech*-en fun | You can vomit from |
| *dem.* | dem. | this. |

Me zol did trogn un	Me zol did trog-en un	May prayers be
zingn	zing-en.	offered up for your
		soul.

Literally means: May you be carried away amidst song.

Yiddish	How You Say It	English
Me zol din aynladn tsum gubernator oyf a seydeh in du zolst im gebn a grepts in ponem arayn.	Me zol din ayn-*lad*-en gu-*ber*-na-tor oyf *sey*-deh in du zolst im gebn a *grepts* in pon-em a-rhine.	May you be invited to a feast by the governor and may you belch in his face.
Me zol rufn tsu dir srotshne a dokter un az iener vet kumen zol men im zogn az me darf shoyn nit.	Me zol *ruf*-en tsu dir *srotsh*-ne a *dok*-ter un az i-*en*-er vet *ku*-men zol men im *zog*-n az me darf *shoy*-en nit.	May someone call a doctor for you urgently, and when he arrives, they should inform him that it is too late.

Megillah	Me-*gil*-lah	Long-winded story

When someone blows something way out of proportion, you can call it a big *megillah*. It's also used to express that someone has told you the entire story with complete details—many times in a very long-winded way. The word actually is the name of the story of Esther and read on the holiday of Purim.

Mensch	*Mensch*	Mensch

Someone who does good works and helps others is called a *mensch*. Literally it means: Person or human being. Use this word when you want to give others the impression that someone is truly worthy of respect for his good deeds, would make a good husband or business partner, treats others fairly and meets his obligations.

Mer vi dayn kop zol id nit onvern.	Mer vi *dayn kop* zol id nit on-vern.	May I not lose anything more than your head.

Meshugeh zolstu vern un orumloyfn iber dee gasn.	Me-*shug*-eh *zols*-tu vern un o-*rum*-loyf-en i-ber dee *gas*-en.	May you go crazy and run around the streets.

Meshugener mamzer	Meh-*shu*-gen-er *mam*-zer.	Crazy bastard

Its roots are from the Hebrew word *meshugga* (meh-*shu*-ga), meaning crazy, and *mamzer*, meaning bastard.

Yiddish	How You Say It	English

Miesseh meshuneh   *Meese*-eh ma-*shee*-neh   An ugly ending to you
Also means: To wish lots of trouble on someone.
Literally means: A strange death or a tragic end.

Migulgl zol er vern in a henglayhter, bay tog zol er hengn, un bay nacht zol er brenen.	Mi-*gul*-gel zol er *vern* in a heng-*layht*-er, bay to zol er *heng*-en, un bay *nacht* zol er bren-en.	He should be transformed into a chandelier, to hang by day and to burn by night.
Mish zich nisht arayn.	*Mish* zich *nisht* a-*rhine*.	Don't butt in. Keep you nose out of it.

Mishegass   Mih-sheh-gas.   Insane or crazy
When everything is just crazy or gone insane, you can call it a big mis*hegass*. This is a variation of the Hebrew word *meshugga* (meh-*shu*-ga), which means crazy.

Mishmash   Mish-*mash*   Mess
When everything is a mess, you can call it a *mishmash*. Also fits when you think something is a hodgepodge or a jumble. It is believed this comes from the fifteenth century and was formed by a repetition of the word *mash*.

Mit a gutn gast frayt men zich ven er kumt arayn; mit a shlechtn gast, ven er gayt avek.	Mit gu-*ten* gas *frayt* men zich ven er *kumt* a-*rhine*; mit a *shlecht*-en gast, ven er *gayt* a-vek.	With a good guest, you are happy when he arrives; with a bad one, when he leaves.
Mit gelt tor men nit stolzyern, veyl me ken es gleych farleyren.	Mit gelt or men nit *stolz*-yer-en, veyl me ken es *gleych* far-*leyr*-en.	Don't boast of money because you can easily lose it.
Mit zechus oves batsolt men nit kayn choyves.	Mit *zach*-us oves bat-solt men nit *kayn* choy-ves.	You cannot pay a debt with a noble pedigree.

Yiddish	How You Say It	English
Mitn malechamo'ves zolstu zid shpeln.	*Mit-*en ma-*lech*-a-mo'ves *zols*-tu zid *shpel-*en.	May you romp with the Angel of Death.
Mitzvah	*Mits*-veh	Good deed

Means: A good deed. When you do something to help someone else, it's called a *mitzvah*.

| *Mosser* | *Moo-*ser | Informer |
| *Naches* | *Nach*-es | Joy |

Means: Joy or happiness. Used most often by parents to say their children give them great *naches*.

| *Nash or nashn* | *Nash* | Nosh |

Light snack or light meal. This comes from the Yiddish word *nash* or *nashn*, which means to eat sweats or to nibble on food. Its origin can be found in the Middle High German word *naschen*, which means to nibble.

| *Nebach* | *Neb-*ach | Pitiable person |
| *Nebbish* | *Neb-*ish | Weakling |

Also a pitiable person but not as bad as a nebach.

| *Nem zich a vaneh.* | Nem zich a *van-*eh. | Go jump in a lake. |

Literally means: Go take a bath.

| *Nezunt un shtark zolstu zayn vee ayzn, zolst zid nit kenen.* | Ne-*zunt* un shtark *zols*-tu zayn vee *ayz-*en *zolst* zid nit *ken-*en. | May you be healthy and tough as iron, so much so that you cannot bend over. |
| *Nit derlebn zolstu eltertsu vern.* | Nit der-*leb-*en *zols*-tu el-*ter*-tsu vern. | May you never become old. |

Yiddish	How You Say It	English
Nit gedacht zolstu vern.	Nit ge-*dacht* zols-tu vern.	May you never be remembered.
Nit hobn zolstu keyn guts in stub.	Nit *hob*-en zols-tu *key*-en guts in *stub.*	May you never enjoy any goodness in your home.
Nit hobn zolstu keyn guts vayl du lebst.	Nit *hob*-en zols-tu *key*-en guts *vayl* du *lebst.*	May you never have anything good all your life.
Nu	*Nu*	What's new?

Nu is a commonly used Yiddish slang for "What's new?" but has many other uses as well. It can also be used as a question, such as: "*Nu?* When does he show up?"; to show impatience, such as "*Nu!* What was said?"; to dare someone, "*Nu*, prove it to me!"; or to just make a strong statement, "*Nu*, I told you so!"

Nudjen	*Nud*-jen	Nudge

Pester or bore. Someone who pesters, annoys or complains persistently. Its origins are from the Polish word *nudzi*, which means the same.

Nudnik	*Nood*-nik	Nudnik; annoying person

If someone is badgering you and they are a very annoying person, you can call them a *nudnik*. Also used when someone is a bore, being obnoxious, nagging you, or generally being a nuisance.

Opkenumen zoln dir dee hent vern.	Op-*ken*-u-men zoln dir dee *hent vern.*	May your arms and hands be paralyzed.
Orem iz nit kayn shand, ober oych kayn groisser koved nit.	O-*rem* iz nit *kayn shande*, o-*ber* oych kayn *grois*-er *kov*-ed nit.	Poverty is no disgrace, but also no great honor.

Yiddish	How You Say It	English
Oy gevalt.	*Oy* ge-*valt.*	Holy shit.

Use it when you hear shocking news. It's usually used to express alarm, dismay, fear, terror or astonishment. When used with "*Oy,*" it can mean "That's dreadful!" or "Holy shit!" The Yiddish origin is the word *G'vald,* which means force or violence.

Oy vay.	*Oy* vay.	Oh, no.

Oy vay means Oh, no, but in Yiddish actually means Oh, woe. People also use it to say things like, "How terrible," or "That's horrible."

Oyb du zogst lign zolstu krenk lign.	Oyb du *zogst* li-*gen* zols-tu *krenk* li-*gen.*	If you tell a lie may you lie ill.
Oyf doktoyrim zol er dos avekgebn.	Oyf *dok*-toy-rim zol er dos a-*vek*-geb-en.	He should give it all away to doctors.
Oyf keyn guten-ort zolstu nit shteyn nor lign.	Oyf *keyn gut*-en-ort zols-tu nit *shtey*-en nor *lig*-en.	May you not stand in a cemetery, only lie there.
Oysbrechen zolstu dee hent mit dee fus.	Oys-*brech*-en *zols*-tu dee *hent* mit dee *foos.*	May you break your arms and your legs.
Oysgefleekt zolstu vern.	Oys-*gef*-leekt *zols*-tu vern.	May suffering consume you.
Oyskrenkn zolstu alts vos du farmogst un farzetsn der vaybs spodnitse.	Oys-*krenk*-en *zols*-tu alts vos du far-*mogst* un far-*zets*-en der *vayb*-es spod-*nit*-se.	May sickness drain all you have and may you pawn your wife's skirt.
Oyskrinkn zol er dus mame's milach.	Oy-*strink*-en zol er dus *ma*-me's *mil*-ach.	He should get so sick as to cough up his mother's milk.
Paygeren zol er.	Pay-*ger*-en zol er.	He should drop dead.

Yiddish	How You Say It	English

Pisher   *Pish*-er   Inexperienced person
Also can be used to indicate someone is inexperienced, unseasoned or "wet behind the ears." Or for someone who thinks he's adult enough to handle a task, but really isn't. Another more literal meaning is bed-wetter.

Platsn zolstu fun   *Plats*-en *zols*-tu fun   May you explode from
naches.   *nach*-es.   pleasure.

Plotz   *Plots*   Burst
When you feel like you are ready to explode from too much excitement or anger, you can say, "I want to *plotz*."

Poyer   *Poy*-er   Dull-witted
Also can refer to a peasant, farmer, boor or dullard

Putz   *Putz*   Fool or idiot

Rugelach   Ru-*ge*-lach   Rugelach
Crescent-shaped cookie made from a cream-cheese dough filled with jam, chocolate, cinnamon, sugar or nuts, or some combination of these ingredients, cut into a triangle and rolled up.

S'zol did onchapn a   S'zol did on-*chap*-en a   May you feel pricks,
shtechenish un a   *shtech*-en-ish un a   bites, aching bones
brechenish, a raysenish   *brech*-en-ish, a *ryas*-   and sores all over your
un a baysenish.   en-ish una *bays*-en-ish.   body

S'zol dir dreyn in boyd.   *S'zol* dir *drey*-en in   May you have a
    boyd.   revolution in your
      stomach.

S'zol dir shnaydn bay   S'zol dir *shnayd*-en bay   May you have terrible
di kishkes.   di *keesh*-kes.   stabbing pains in your
      bowels.

S'zol dir vaksn a   S'zol dir *vaks*-en a   May a boil grow on
geshver oyfn pupik.   *gesh*-ver oyf-en *poo*-   your belly button.
    pik.

Yiddish	How You Say It	English

Saichel   *Say*-chel   Wise

When you think someone is very smart or wise, you say they have *saichel*. This can also mean: Someone has common sense, tact or diplomacy.

Sazol dir azoy dreyen   *Sa*-zol dir a-zoy *drey*-en   May your innards turn
boyd me zol meynen   *boyd* me zol *mey*-nen   and grind so much,
az sayiz a katerinke.   az *say*-iz a ka-*ter*-in-ke.   people will think you
                                                            are an organ grinder.

Schmir   *Schmeer*   Schmear

To use a dab of cream cheese is one common meaning, but you will also hear *shmear* used when people talk about buying a bunch of things together, such as "She bought the whole *shmear*." The Yiddish word *schmir* means smear or smudge, from the word *shmirn* or grease, which stems from the Middle High German word *smiren,* also meaning to smear or grease. When not used in the context of eating, *shmear* can mean the whole works or to be excessively kind for selfish gains.

Shalom   *Sha*-lom   Hello

Hebrew word with lots of different meanings, including, hello, peace, good-bye, so long, and other similar words of welcome when someone comes in, or good-bye when someone leaves. But it's only good-bye until you can welcome someone again.

Shandeh   *Shan*-deh   Shame

Use when you are embarrassed about something or think something is a shame.

Shikker   *Shik*-er   Drunkard

Someone who is a drunkard, is a *shikker.* Its origins are in the Hebrew word *sikkor* or *sakar,* "to be drunk."

Shlak   *Shlak*   Shlock joint

Junk shop or has no value. Literally it means evil. When you go into a store that sells cheap stuff, you can call it a "*shlok* joint." Its origins is the Middle High German word *slag.*

Yiddish	How You Say It	English

Shlemazel   *Shleh-mah*-zel   Incompetent person
Also can refer to someone who has perpetual bad luck or misfortune.

Shlemiel   Shleh-*meal*   Butter-fingered
Also an inept or foolish person, a simpleton, nincompoop or a bungler.

Shlepn   *Shlep*-en   Shlep
Means to drag an object with difficulty. It can also be used for a long, tedious or difficult journey. Like, "Wasn't that trip to the city a *shlep*?" Its origins are the German word *schleppen*, which means "to drag."

Shlepper   Shlep-per   Sponger
Also can refer to someone who always tags along or a jerk.

Shlog zich kog in vant.   *Shlog zich kog in vant.*   Go break you own head.

Shlump   *Shloomp*   Poor dresser
Also unstylish or with bad posture. When a someone corrects another because his shoulders are drooping, they can say "Don't *shlump*!"

Shlumpf   *Shlumpf*   Sucker
Also a patsy, fall guy or second rater.

Shmaltz   Shmaltz   Greasy
Melted fat. Usually used to refer to something that is greasy, gooey or has lots of fat drippings. But, you'll also hear it when someone is talking about something corny or overly sentimental. In that case a "y" is added at the end. For example, "Wasn't that a *shmaltzy* play?" Some people also use *shmaltzy* to describe something as flattery, sweet talk or overpraise. For example, "Wasn't that a *shmaltzy* introduction?" Its origins are in the German word *schmaltz* of the same meaning.

Yiddish	How You Say It	English

Shmegegi   Shmeh-*geh*-gee   Idiot
Also a nothing or a nobody.

Shmok   *Shmok*   Shmo
If you think someone is a complete jerk or patsy, you can call him a *shmo*. It comes from the Yiddish word *shmok*, which means penis or fool.

Shmuck   *Shmuck*   Clumsy person
Shmuck means a clumsy or stupid person. This comes from the Yiddish word *shmock*, which means penis or fool, but some think its beginnings are actually in the Polish word *smok*, which means serpent or tail.

Shmuck   *Shmuck*   Self-made fool
Also dickhead, idiot or jerk. Another word for penis.
Literally means: Jewel.

Shmuesn   Shmues-en   Schmooze
Engage in casual conversation, many times in order to gain an advantage or make a social connection. The Yiddish word *shmuesn* has its origins both in *shmues* (chat) or *schmue* (rumor).

Shmutz   *Shmutz*   Dirt
Lots of dirt or slime.

Shnoits   *Shnoyts*   Shnoz
Nose, which comes from the Yiddish word *shnoits*, which means snout.

Shnook   *Shnook*   Shnook
When someone is easily victimized, in other words stupid, a sucker or a dupe, you can call them a *shnook*. Its origins are in the Lithuanian word *snukis*, which means mug or snout.

Shnorrer   *Shnor*-er   Panhandler
Also can refer to a beggar, moocher or freeloader. *Shnorrers* make a career of panhandling and think they were doing others a favor by allowing them to do a *mitzvah* (good deed) through donating to the needy.

Yiddish	How You Say It	English

Shoyn opgetrent?   *Shoin op-*geh-trent?   Finished fucking?

Also translates to: Are you finished screwing around? Or, Have you finished the dirty work?

Literally means: Have you finished fornicating?

Shraybn zol men dir	*Shrayb-*en zol men dir	If anyone writes you,
retseptn.	re-*tsept-*en.	they should write you
		doctors' prescriptions.

| *Shteyner ayf zayne* | *Shteyn-*er ayf *zayne* | Stones on his bones. |
| *bainer.* | *bain-*er. | |

Shteyner zol zi hoben,	*Shtey-*ner zol zi *hob-*en,	She should have
nit kayn kinder.	nit *kayn kin-*der.	stones and not
		children.

Shtik   *Shtik*   Comedy act

Piece or routine. An entertainment routine, usually a comedy act. Its origins are from the High Middle German word *stucke* or piece.

Shtik drek   *Shtick* drek   Piece of shit

Shtinker   *Shtink-*er   Smelly person

Also can refer to someone who behaves offensively.

Shtup es in toches.   *Shtoop* es in *too-*ches.   Shove it up your ass.

Shvitzer   *Shvitz-*er   Braggart

Literally means: Someone who sweats.

Strasheh mich nit.   *Stra-*sheh mich nit.   Don't threaten me.

Ti mir eppes.	*Tee* mir ep-is.	So what do you think
		you can do to me?
		Nothing.

Toches ahfen tish.   *Too-*ches *ah-*fin *tish.*   Put up or shut up.

Also can be used to mean: Let's conclude this! Or Come clean, buddy! Literally means: Put your buttocks on the table!

Yiddish	How You Say It	English

Toches-lecker — Too-ches leck-er — Ass kisser
Also can refer to a brown-noser or someone who will do anything to gain favor.
Literally means: buttock-licker.

Tough *toches* — Too-ches — Tough luck
Literally means tough ass. Use when you want to say tough luck or too bad. *Toches* is another word for butt, ass, backside or fanny. You get the idea.

Traif — *Trayf* — Unkosher
Forbidden food and not prepared by the rules of Jewish dietary laws. It's the opposite of kosher. You may hear this word also used for non-food items, such as books or movies, that are forbidden. For example, "Don't go to see, *Deep Throat* [a pornographic flick]—it's *traif.*"

Trinkn zoln im piavkes — *Trink*-en zoln im piav-kes. — Leeches should drink him dry.

Trogn zol dir der ruech oyf di pleytses. — *Trog*-en zol dir der *ru*-ech oyf di *pleyts*-es. — May the Devil carry you on his shoulders.

Trogn zol men dir oyf der miteh. — *Trog*-en zol men dir oyf der *mit*-eh. — May you be carried out on a dead man's stretcher.

Tsap mir nit dos blut. — *Tsap* meer nit dos blut — Don't aggravate me.
Literally means: Don't bleed me.

Tseboyechen zolstu ruk-un-lend. — Tse-*boy*-ech-en *zols*-tu ruk-un-*lend*. — May you break all your bones.
Literally means: May you break your back and your sides.

Tsen shifn mit gold zol er farmorgn, un dos gantse gelt zol er farkrenkn. — *Tsen shif*-en mit gold zol er far-*morg*-en un does *gant*-se getl zol er far-krenk-en. — Ten ships of gold should be his and the money should only make him sick.

Yiddish	How You Say It	English
Tsen shifn mit gold zolstu farmogn in dos gantse gelt zolstu farkrenkn.	Tsen *shif*-en mit gold *zols*-tu far-*mog*-en in do *gant*-se *gelt zols*-tu far-*kenk*-en.	May you own ten ships full of gold and may you spend it all on your illnesses.
Tsi bistu meshugeh?	Tsi-*bis*-tu me-*shug*-eh?	Are you crazy?
Tsores	*Sor*-es	Troubles

When you have a lot of problems or troubles, you can say you are facing a lot of *tsores.* Also can be used to express misery.

Tzatzkeh	*Tzatz*-keh	Bimbo

Also can refer to someone who is a mistress, sexually attractive girl, or an overdressed woman. Another meaning can be a toy, ornament or expensive plaything.

Varfn zol did eylenvayz.	Var-*fen* zol did ey-*len*-wayz.	A fever should toss you (in bed) a foot high each time.
Vemen barestu?	*Vay*-men bar-es-tu?	Who are you kidding, who do you think you are screwing around with?

Literally means: Who are you screwing?

Ven hungert a nogid? Ven der doktor hayst im.	Ven *hung*-ert a *nog*-d? Ven der *dokt*-or *hayst* im.	When does a wealthy man go hungry? When the doctor orders him.
Ver bagrobn nayn eyln in der erd.	Ver ba-*grog*-en *nayn eyl*-en in der erd.	May you be buried nine feet deep in the ground.
Ver derharget.	*Ver* der-*har*-get.	Drop dead.

Also can mean: Bury yourself. Go kill yourself.

Yiddish	How You Say It	English
Ver dershtikt.	*Vair* der-shtikt.	Choke on it.
Ver es varft oil yenem shteyner krigt tsurik in di aigneh bainer.	Ver es *varft* oil *yen*-em *shteyn*-er krigt *tsur*-ik in di *aig*-neh *bain*-er.	He who throws stones on another gets them back on his own bones.
Ver farblondjet.	*Vair* far-*blond*-jet.	Get lost.
Verem essn toiterhayt un deiges lebedikerhayt.	Ve-*rem* es-sen toi-*ter*-hayt un *dei*-ges le-*bed*-i-ker-*hayt.*	Worms eat you up when dead and worries eat you up alive.
Vern zol fun did a blintshik in fun is a kats. Er sol did oyfesn un mit dir zin der-vargn—volt men fun ayn beydn ptur gevorn.	*Vern* zol fun did a *blint*-shik in fun is a *kats.* Er sol did *oyf*-esn un mit dir zin der-*varg*-en—*volt* men fun ayn *beyd*-en *ptur* ge-vorn.	May you turn into a pancake and he into a cat. He should eat you and choke on you—that way we will be rid of both of you.
Vern zol fun dir a blintshik in dee kats zol did chapn.	*Vern* zol fun dir a *blint*-shik in de *kats* zol di chapn.	May you turn into a pancake and be snatched away by the cat
Vest vellen zich oysfaynen far layt, vestu shtarbn far der tsayt.	*Vest vell*-en zich oys-*fay*-nen far *layt, ves*-tu shtrab-en far der *tsayt.*	If you want to please everybody, you'll die before your time.
Vi me bet zich oys, azoy darf men shlofn.	Vi me bet *zich* oys, a-*zoy* darf men *shlof*-en.	As you make your bed, so will you sleep in it.
Vi tsu derleb ich im shoyn tsu bagrobn.	Vi tsu *der*-leb ich im *shoy*-en tsu ba-*grob*-en.	I should outlive him long enough to bury him.

Yiddish	How You Say It	English
Vifil yor er iz gegangn oyf di fis zol er geyn af di hent un di iberike zol er zich sharn oyf di hintn.	Vi-fil yor er iz ge-*gang*-en oyf di fis zol er geyn af hi *hent* un di i-*ber*-ike zol er zich *sharn* oyf di *hint*-en.	As many years as he's walked on his feet, let him walk on his hands, and for the rest of the time he should crawl along on his ass.

Yenta	*Yen*-teh	Gossip

Also can refer to someone who is a busybody, talkative woman or blabbermouth.

Yentzer	*Yents*-er	Pimp

Also, someone who will screw you in a nonsexual way.

Zalts im in di oygen, feffer im in di noz.	*Zalts* im in di *oyg*-en, *fef*-er im in di *noz*.	Throw salt in his eyes, pepper in his nose.

Zayn mazel zol im layhtn vee dee levone in sof choydesh.	*Zayn maz*-el zol im *layht*-en vee dee *lev*-one in *sof choy*-desh.	His luck should be as bright as a new moon.

Zei nit kain vyzoso.	*Zye* nit kane vi-*zo*-so.	Don't be an idiot.

Also can mean: Don't be a damn fool. or Don't be a penis.

Zeit nit kain goylem.	*Zye* nit kane *go*-lem.	Don't be a fool.

Also can mean: Don't be a robot.

Zeit nit kain nar.	*Zye* nit kane *nar*.	Don't be a fool.

Zhlob	*Zhlob*	Slob

Also someone who is clumsy, uncouth or foolish.

Zol dich chappen beim boych.	Zol dich *chap*-in byme boych.	You should only get a stomach cramp.

Yiddish	How You Say It	English
Zol dir got arayngebn a naye neshumah un tsuhemen di alte.	Zol dir got a-*rhine*-geb-en a *naye* ne-*shum*-ah un tsu-*hem*-en di *al*-the.	Drop dead.

Literally means: May God give you a new soul and take your old one.

Zol dir grihmen in boych.	Zol dir *grih*-min in boych.	You should get a stomach cramp.
Zol dir vaksn tzibbeles fun pupik.	Zol dir *vox*-en *tzib*-eh-les fun *poop*-ik.	Onions should grow on your navel.
Zol er tzebrechne a fus.	Zol er tze-*brech*-en a foos.	He should break a leg.
Zol es brennen.	Zol es *bren*-in.	To hell with it.
Zol es dir aroys bokem.	Zol es dir a-*roys* bok-em.	May it end badly for you.
Zol es im onkumn vos ich vintsh im [chotsh a helft, chotsh halb, chotsh a tsent cheyli].	Zol es im on-*kumn* vos ich *vintsh* im [*chotsh* a *helft*, chotsh *halb*, *chotsh* a tsent chey-li].	Let what I wish on him come true [most, even half, even just 10 [percent.]
Zol shoyn zany a groyser irid in gen-eden, un zolst dortn matslich shem.	Zol *shoyn* za-ny a *groys*-er i-*rid* in gen-e-den un zolst *dort*-en *mats*-lich shem.	May there be a great fair in Paradise and may you be very successful there.
Zoln dayn kishkes farfrayrn vern oyf azoy fil, az nor der fyer fun gehnum zol zey kenen tseshmeltsn	Zoln *dayn kish*-kes far-*frayr*-en vern oyf a-*zoy* fil, az nor der *fy*-er fun *geh*-num zol zey ken-en. tsesh-*melt*-sen.	May your guts freeze so hard that only hellfire will be able to thaw them.

Yiddish	How You Say It	English
Zoln dayne shunim oyslenkn zeyere fim ven zey veln tantsn oyf dayn keyver.	Zoln *day*-ne *shun*-im oys-*len*-ken *zey*-ere fim ven zey *veln tants*-en oyf dayn *key*-ver.	May your enemies sprain their ankles dancing on your grave.
Zoln dir vaksn burekes fun pupik, in zolst pishn mit borsht.	*Zoln* dir *vaks*-en bu-*rek*-es fun *pup*-ik in *zolst pish*-en mit *borsht*.	May a red beet grow out of your belly button, and may you pee borsht.
Zoln verem praven a chaseneh in dayn boyn in aynladn ale zeyere kroyvim fun inupets biz sladobke.	Zoln *ver*-em *prav*-en a *chas*-e-neh in dayn boyn in ayn-*lad*-en ale *zey*-ere *kroy*-vim fun in-u-*pets* biz *slad*-ob-ke.	May worms hold a wedding in your stomach and invite their relatives from all over.
Zolst azoy farfoylt vern az tsign, tchoyrn, un chazirim zoln zid opzogn tsu forn mit dir in eyn fur.	Zolst a-*zoy far*-foylt vern az *tsign*, *tchoy*-ern un cha-*zir*-im zoln zid op-*zog*-en tsu *forn* mit dir in eyn fur.	May you rot so badly that goats, skunks and pigs will decline to travel in the same cart as you.
Zolst azoy seyn redn az nor di kats zoln dir farshteyn.	Zolst a-*zoy sey*-en *red*-en az nor *kats zoln* dir *farsht*-eyn.	May you speak so eloquently that only a cat will understand you.
Zolst beser lebn un mutshen zid.	*Zolst bes*-er *leb*-en un mut-*shen* zid.	Better that you should live and suffer.
Zolst es shtupin in toches arayn.	Zolst es *shtoop*-en in *too*-ches a-rhine.	You should shove it up your ass.
Zolst farshporn di bizoynut un di krenh fun der elter.	*Zolst* far-*shpor*-en di bi-*zoyn*-ut un *kren*-eh fun der *elt*-er.	May you be spared the indignities and illnesses of old age.
Zolst geshvollen veren vi a barg.	Zolst geh-*shvol*-en *ver*-en vi a barg.	You should swell up like a mountain.

Yiddish	How You Say It	English
Zolst hobn di same fete gandz—nor kit keyn tseyner di beste vayn nor nit keyn chushtem di senste vayb - nor nit keyn zehrut.	Zolst *hob*-en di sa-*me* fete *gandz*—nor kit *key*-en *tseyn*-er; di *bes*-te *vine* nor nit keyn *chush*-tem; di *sens*-te *vayb*—nor nit *key*-en *zeh*-rut.	May you have the juiciest goose—but no teeth; the best wine— but no sense of taste; the most beautiful wife—but be impotent.
Zolst hobn hano'ie fun dayn chuneh-seudeh un zid dervargn mit letstn bisn.	*Zolst hob*-en ha-*no*'ie fun *dayn chun*-eh *seu*-deh un zid der-*varg*-en mit *letst*-en *bis*-en.	May you enjoy your wedding breakfast and choke on your last bite.
Zolst lebn biz hoondert un tsvantseek yor—mit a heeltsernem kop in glezerne oygn.	Zolst *leb*-en biz *hoond*-ert un *tsvants*-eek yor—mit a *heel-tser*-nem kop in *glez*-erne *oyg*-en.	May you live until one hundred and twenty— with a wooden head and glass eyes.
Zolst lign in drerd.	Zolst *lig*-en in *drerd.*	Drop dead.
Zolst syn vee a lump: hengen by tog, brenen by nacht in oysgeyn zolstu in der fri.	Zolst syn vee a *lump*: *heng*-en by *to*, *bren*-en by *nacht* in oys-geyn *zols*-tu in der fri.	May you be a lamp: hang by day, burn by night and be snuffed out in the morning.
Zolst vern azoy rayd almo'nes man zol zid keyn mol nit zorgen vegn perno'se.	Zolst vern a-*zoy rayd* almo'nes man zol zid *keyn* mol nit *zorg*-en veg-en per-*no*-se.	May you become so rich that your widow's husband should never have any worries about his livelihood.
Zolst zid azoy matern mitn toyt vee in mater zid.	Zolst zid a-*zoy* ma-*tern mit*-en *toyt* vee in ma-*ter* zid.	May you be as tormented in your death as I am in my life.